NATURAL THEOLOGY

NATURAL THEOLOGY

Geerhardus Vos

Translated by Albert Gootjes
Introduced by J. V. Fesko

Reformation Heritage Books
Grand Rapids, Michigan

Reformation Heritage Books
3070 29th St. SE
Grand Rapids, MI 49512
616-977-0889
orders@heritagebooks.org
www.heritagebooks.org

Special thanks to Heritage Hall archive at the Hekman Library, Calvin Seminary and University, for use of the manuscripts needed to create this book.

Printed in the United States of America
22 23 24 25 26 27/10 9 8 7 6 5 4 3 2 1

Library of Congress Cataloging-in-Publication Data

Names: Vos, Geerhardus, 1862-1949, author. | Gootjes, Albert, translator.
Title: Natural theology / Geerhardus Vos ; translated by Albert Gootjes ; introduced by J. V. Fesko.
Description: Grand Rapids, Michigan : Reformation Heritage Books, [2022] | Includes bibliographical references and index.
Identifiers: LCCN 2021043235 (print) | LCCN 2021043236 (ebook) | ISBN 9781601789082 (hardcover) | ISBN 9781601789099 (epub)
Subjects: LCSH: Theology, Doctrinal. | Natural theology. | BISAC: RELIGION / Christian Theology / Systematic
Classification: LCC BT22 .V67 2022 (print) | LCC BT22 (ebook) | DDC 230—dc23
LC record available at https://lccn.loc.gov/2021043235
LC ebook record available at https://lccn.loc.gov/2021043236

For additional Reformed literature, request a free book list from Reformation Heritage Books at the above regular or email address.

CONTENTS

FOREWORD

Geerhardus Vos has long been recognized as a significant figure in American Reformed theology, best known for his various published works on biblical theology. A revival of interest in Vos's thought during the past two decades has brought to light his correspondence, his work on Old Testament eschatology, and most recently his four-volume *Reformed Dogmatics*.[1] The volumes of Vos's dogmatics, originally in the form of lectures delivered in Dutch, were transcribed by students, and later made available in mimeographed form, both of a handwritten text and of a typed version. These and other theological texts from the late nineteenth and early twentieth centuries reside in the Heritage Hall archives at Calvin Seminary and University.

In 2017, James Baird, then engaged in graduate study at the Free University in Amsterdam on Vos's covenantal ethics and anthropology, examined the archival holdings in Heritage Hall and identified the Vos manuscripts on natural theology. He also argued the desirability of a translation of these materials. His examination of the archival materials revealed one fragmentary and two complete manuscript versions of Vos's lectures on natural theology. Given the dates on the two complete texts, these transcripts are either student notes on dictated lectures delivered by someone other than Vos or transcripts of earlier manuscripts of Vos's lectures—all copied after Vos's departure to Princeton Seminary. The archives do not contain any earlier versions of the lectures.

It is worth noting that this pattern of dictating fairly well-formed lectures and of preparing and preserving transcriptions, sometimes as

1. Geerhardus Vos, *Reformed Dogmatics*, trans. and ed. Richard B. Gaffin Jr. et al., 5 vols. (Bellingham, Wash.: Lexham, 2012–2016).

the basis for further publication, whether in mimeographed form or in a printed text, was fairly common in the era. Abraham Kuyper's five-volume dogmatics is itself a *Dictaten*, transcribed and later published.[2] It was also such a process that led to the final published form of Louis Berkhof's famous *Systematic Theology*.

The present translation of Vos's lectures on natural theology by Albert Gootjes, with introduction by John Fesko, brings to light a significant aspect of Geerhardus Vos's work. Albeit comparatively brief, the lectures evidence Vos's acquaintance with the older Reformed orthodox approaches to natural theology and his extensive knowledge of relevant developments in nineteenth-century thought. Although the dates on the extant manuscripts indicate that they were produced in 1895 and 1898, Vos's original lectures were certainly delivered between 1888 and 1893 when he was professor of theology at the Theological School of the Christian Reformed Church in Grand Rapids, Michigan, in all probability contemporaneously with his lectures on dogmatics, which were published in mimeographed form in 1896, after Vos had moved to Princeton and close to the date of the natural theology transcripts. Transcriptions of both sets of Vos's lectures, then, were used after his departure. The difference is that the transcriptions of the dogmatic lectures went through a more extensive process than the lectures on natural theology, culminating in mimeographed publication. The two sets of Vos's lectures—the natural theology and the dogmatics—are also similar in format: both take the form of question and answer, echoing the catechetical mode of the original theological text used in the Theological School, namely, Aegidius Francken's *Kern der Christelijke Leer*.[3]

Given the similarity of form and inasmuch as Vos's *Reformed Dogmatics* lack a prolegomenon, a case could be made that the lectures on natural theology might have served as an introduction or part of an introduction. They include discussion of religion and of proofs of the

2. Abraham Kuyper, *Dictaten Dogmatiek: College-dictaat van een der Studenten*, 5 vols. (Kampen: J. H. Kok, 1910).

3. Aegidius Francken, *Kern der Christelijke Leer: dat is de waarheden van de Hervormde godsdienst, eenvoudig ter nedergesteld, en met de oefening der ware Godzaligheid aangedrongen* (Dordrecht: J. van Braam, 1713; Groningen: O. L. Schildkamp, 1862).

existence of God, characteristic of the prolegomenal portions of various late orthodox theologies, and they include also a rebuttal of pantheism, an issue that also arises briefly at the beginning of the lectures on dogmatics. Even if this suggestion of a connection between the two sets of lectures does not prove convincing, publication of Vos's lectures on natural theology does fill out the picture of the scope of his dogmatic or doctrinal theology and of his knowledge of nineteenth-century theological and philosophical developments. Hopefully, this publication will serve to stimulate interest in Reformed theological development at the turn of the twentieth century, in much-needed archival work, and potentially in further translation of previously unpublished works by Vos and his contemporaries.

Richard A. Muller
Lowell, Michigan

TRANSLATOR'S PREFACE

The Manuscripts

Vos's lectures on natural theology survive in three sets of student dictation notes, all currently held in Heritage Hall of the Hekman Library at Calvin University in Grand Rapids, Michigan. Two of the three are complete.[1] The first (siglum: DG), written in a fair hand, is signed "13 April 10 PM 95. Grand Rapids Mich. W. de Groot." Willem de Groot (1872–1955) received his diploma from the Theological School in Grand Rapids in 1897 and was awarded a Th.M. from Princeton Seminary in 1918. He served as a home missionary and, while engaged in that work in Chicago from 1918 to 1919, he studied briefly at the University of Chicago. The lecture notes taken down by De Groot are distinguished in that they represent the only copy to include a table of contents and section headings. The colophon to the second copy (siglum: V) reads: "27. Sept. 1898. L. J. Veltkamp. Grand Rapids Mich." Lambertus Veltkamp (1876–1952) received his diploma from the Theological School in 1901 and served as a minister from that year until his retirement in 1942. Like DG, the hand in V is fair. In fact, there is little doubt that V is a neat copy taken from a rough draft. This is suggested not only by the neat hand, but also by the fact that the notebook containing the lectures on natural theology continues immediately with Veltkamp's dictation notes of Vos's lectures on hermeneutics, tidily separated by a blank page bearing the title of this new section.

1. All three manuscripts are found in the "Geerhardus Vos Collection, ID: COLL/319, Series 1, Box 4, Folder 1," in Heritage Hall archive at the Hekman Library, Calvin Seminary and University, Grand Rapids, Michigan.

To these two manuscript copies one can add a third, incomplete set of dictation notes (siglum: A). With the text ending abruptly after question 154 (thus omitting the response), A may not be entirely complete, but still preserves roughly two-thirds of the text. Unlike DG and V, A includes no indication of who the student recording the lectures was, nor has it been possible to identify him by his hand, which may be legible but is considerably more difficult to decipher than that of the other two. The lectures on natural theology in A are followed by a single blank leaf, after which we find dictation notes of New Testament exegesis lectures—from the same hand—beginning somewhere in the middle of verse 4 of Ephesians 1 and ending equally abruptly in its discussion of verse 9. After another blank leaf, one finds another three leaves containing four and a half pages of Old Testament exegesis dictation notes on the last two verses of Psalm 2. The unidentified student recorded the lectures beginning on the page facing the inside back cover, such that the notes on Psalm 2 are upside down and backward relative to the lectures on natural theology and on Ephesians 1. Although these notes do take us to the end of Psalm 2, they begin abruptly in verse 11 with "This forms a stark contrast with what..." (*Dit vormt een sterke tegenstelling met wat...*).

These excerpts from lectures on Old and New Testament exegesis seem to indicate that the unidentified student used the notebook in which A is recorded in class. It is therefore possible that A, unlike V (and perhaps DG, given the section headings unique to it[2]), represents an original rough draft taken down during dictation. Textually, there is greater general agreement between V and A than there is between either one of them and DG. In fact, certain textual variants suggest that there may well be a direct relationship between V and A,[3] although greater study is indeed required to verify this initial claim and, if upheld, to

2. That DG is a copy rather than original dictation notes may likewise be suggested by the temporal indicator "10 PM" in the colophon (see above). That is, it may indicate the time when the De Groot finished copying a manuscript made available to him by another student, rather than the time when the professor finished the series of lectures.

3. See, for example, the blank both V and A leave for the "Hibbert Lectures" in Q. 77.5.b, and the omission by both V and A of the first of two alternatives in regard to Locke in Q. 130.

determine whether V was actually copied from A, whether they rather had a common *Vorlage* (thus meaning that A is not an in-class draft, as suggested above), and so on. Yet the most striking thing about the Vos lectures on natural theology is that the text is actually very stable across DG, V, and A—especially if the extant manuscripts do indeed include both rough draft and neat copy versions, as nineteenth-century students are known to have expanded their rough drafts when they in the evening hours turned them into neat copies for further study.[4] The close textual correspondence suggests that the extant manuscripts bring us very close to Vos's own words, a circumstance which only increases their value for the study of his thought.

The precise genealogy between the three extant manuscripts deserves more extensive exploration than is possible within the confines of the present translation. Of particular interest are the dates recorded in DG (1895) and V (1898). Does the three-year interval separating the notes indicate that Vos's notes were dictated at the Grand Rapids Theological School even in his absence? Or did theological students copy the notes recorded by fellow students and circulate these manuscripts among themselves? These questions are obviously of value in detailing and evaluating the early reception of Vos's natural theology. In any case, the multiple manuscripts and different dates are indicative of a certain interest in Vos's views at the close of the nineteenth century.

Text and Translation

The first draft of the translation presented here was made on the basis of the transcription of V produced by the Dutch student A. Veuger, as part of a master's level thesis on Vos's contribution to the development of Reformed theology in North America.[5] This first translation was

4. An example are the lectures that the nineteenth-century Dutch Protestant theologian J. H. Gunning Jr. (1829–1905) gave on Benedictus Spinoza's *Ethics* from 1887 to 1888, of which the editor had both an original rough draft and an expanded neat copy from a single student available to him. See the discussion in Leo Mietus, introduction to *Over Spinoza's* Ethica: *Collegedictaat opgetekend door Chr. Hunningher: Amsterdam, 1887–1888,* by J. H. Gunning Jr., ed. Leo Mietus (Zoetermeer: Boekencentrum, 2015), 9–10.

5. A. Veuger, "Geerhardus Vos en zijn bijdrage aan de gereformeerde theologie in Amerika: Tekst en context van Vos' colleges over natuurlijke theologie" (master's thesis,

then checked against both DG and A (and, in most cases, also against V itself, given the errors detected in the Veuger transcription), with all variants of some significance being recorded. It was this process of text-critical study, of course, which yielded the above conclusion regarding the stability of the text across the three extant manuscripts. Given both this stability and the ready online accessibility of the Veuger transcription, it was not deemed necessary to produce a critical edition of the original Dutch text of the Vos lectures to accompany the present translation. At the same time, the text-critical work that has been done satisfies the demands of due diligence and moreover gives the reader access to all textual issues of import. Above all, it needs to be emphasized that there really is only a single text and that many of the variants concern an error in dictation or copying which most likely would have been caught and corrected in the process of translation and editing anyway.[6]

Below we therefore present the translation of a "best text"—namely, an eclectic text based primarily on V, but with correct or "best" readings supplied from DG and/or A. Footnotes have been inserted wherever textual variants of some significance occurred. Where the variant consists of more than one word, left and right substitution brackets (⸢ and ⸣) mark the extent of the variant, with a footnote following the closing bracket. Variants consisting of only one word are marked only by a footnote. The notes take the following form, as in this example from Q. 75.3.a:

> V and A: "morality" (*zedelijkheid*); DG: "rationality" (*redelijkheid*)

The footnotes thus first supply the manuscript evidence for the preferred reading as it has been translated in the main text. Following a semicolon, the notes then supply the inferior or alternate reading (or readings), together with the manuscript evidence for it (or them). Textual variants are presented in both English translation and their original Dutch form, since the latter sometimes helps to shed light on the nature

---

Theologische Universiteit Apeldoorn, 2019), accessed April 20, 2020, http://theoluniv.ub.rug.nl/241/1/2019%20Veuger%2C%20A.%20MA.pdf.

6. E.g., the erroneous "finite" (DG) for "infinite" (V and A) in Q. 91, "subjective" (V) for "objective" (DG) in Q. 202.

of the error that occurred. In the example above, for instance, the variant involving the confusion of "morality" and "rationality"—which occurs multiple times—is readily explained by the resemblance between their Dutch counterparts (*zedelijkheid* and *redelijkheid*), especially if one is aware of the similarity between the letters *z* and *r* in late nineteenth-century Dutch handwriting. With very few exceptions, the notes offer no attempt to account for the preferred reading, although cases involving indubitable error are marked as such. The many abbreviations used in the Dutch original have been resolved in the footnotes, except where they form part of the text-critical issue itself or are of significance for interpretation.

Since the underlining in DG, V, and A varies among the manuscripts and is also internally inconsistent, it has not been retained in the translation. For the sake of clarity, the translation has adopted—without notification by way of footnotes—the table of contents and the section headings from DG. As to the numbers for the questions and answers in the course on natural theology, two remarks have to be made. First, for the relative order of the treatment of dualism and polytheism, the translation follows the order in V and A (dualism, QQ. 59–63; polytheism, QQ. 64–68), which has been reversed in DG (polytheism, QQ. 59–63; dualism, QQ. 64–68). This decision was motivated not only by the majority of the manuscript evidence, but also by the fact that the order in V and A follows the order announced in Q. 44 in *all* manuscripts, including DG. Second, in the final third of the manuscript (which is not included in A), the numbering in both DG and V is confused at different places.[7] Since neither manuscript therefore actually numbers the questions entirely correctly, it was decided to depart from both, and to apply our own, correct numbering in the translation.

7. First, in DG the *numbering* skips from 164 to 166, so that there is no 165 in it; while the *text* in DG and V is thus the same, the *numbering* in DG from 166 to 198 is therefore off by one compared to V. The numbering coincides again from 200, since DG omits what in V is question and answer 199. However, following the number 211, V erroneously presents the text on the *identity* theory (212 in DG), thus omitting the text of the question and answer on the *idealist* theory (211 in DG); this is a classic example of error by homoioarcton. Starting at 213, text and numbering in DG and V coincide again, right through to the end.

Finally, in terms of style, the present translation retains the somewhat formal character of Vos's lectures, while giving it a modern hue in terms of sentence structure and vocabulary, so as to make it more palatable to a contemporary readership.

INTRODUCTION

J. V. Fesko

Biblical and natural theology may seem like oil and water, Jerusalem and Athens, or in this case, Geerhardus Vos and Thomas Aquinas. What has one to do with the other? Vos and Aquinas might seem like an ill-matched pair, but the two actually do belong together. As much as Vos has a reputation for being the father of contemporary Reformed biblical theology, he spent his earliest academic labors teaching dogmatics at the Theological School, now Calvin Theological Seminary, in Grand Rapids, Michigan. As a part of his teaching load, Vos taught a course in natural theology, whose lectures appear for the first time in English translation in this volume. Setting the context for Vos's lectures, however, first requires establishing the framework for natural theology in the wider Reformed tradition, more specifically in the nineteenth century, and then within Vos's own education. With Vos's lectures properly framed, the stage is set to delve into the lectures themselves to identify their background, methodology, sources, principles, and relationship to his later thought. This introduction concludes with observations regarding Vos's lectures and the prospects of a revival of a Reformed natural theology.

Natural Theology in the Reformed Tradition

When John Calvin (1509–1564) wrote his treatise *On the Necessity of Reforming the Church,* he identified three key disputed issues between Rome and the Reformation: the doctrine of justification, worship, and church government.[1] As a *reform* movement, Calvin and other Reformers

1. John Calvin, *On the Necessity of Reforming the Church,* trans. Henry Beveridge, in

sought to correct perceived errors, not completely deconstruct and reconstruct theology. In any good history of the Reformation, one must take note of the discontinuities and the continuities between the early modern Protestant churches and their medieval and patristic roots. In this case, one of the continuities lies in the use and promotion of natural theology. Natural revelation is what God reveals through nature, or creation, whereas special revelation is what God reveals through His Word. Natural theology, on the other hand, is the interpretation and systemization of the data of natural revelation. In general, early modern Reformed theologians employed natural theology to varying degrees in their theology, which represents a continuity with the theologians of the patristic era and the Middle Ages.[2]

Augustine (354–430) is an anchor point for the theology of both the Protestant and Roman Catholic traditions. In his famous *City of God* Augustine posited that Platonist philosophers most closely approximated the truth of Christianity, though Plato (ca. 428–348 BC) stood head and shoulders above his disciples.[3] In his estimation, the Platonists "have recognized the true God as the author of all things, the source of the light of truth, and the bountiful bestower of all blessedness."[4] They discern God's nature by perceiving the doctrines of God's immutability and simplicity, and thus conclude that all things must have been made by Him and that He Himself was made by none.[5] In his mind, Augustine's observations about the natural theology of the Platonists echo the teaching of Paul in Romans 1:19–20.[6] But Augustine notes that

Tracts and Letters of John Calvin, ed. Jules Bonnet and Henry Beveridge (repr., Edinburgh: Banner of Truth, 2009), 1:123–236.

2. See Richard A. Muller, *Dictionary of Latin and Greek Theological Terms: Drawn Principally from Protestant Scholastic Theology*, 2nd ed. (Grand Rapids: Baker Academic, 2017), s.v. *theologia naturalis* (pp. 362–63).

3. Augustine, *City of God*, trans. Marcus Dods (1950; repr., New York: Modern Library, 1993), 8.1, 4–5. For what follows, also see Alexander W. Hall, "Natural Theology in the Middle Ages," in *The Oxford Handbook of Natural Theology*, ed. Russell Re Manning (Oxford: Oxford University Press, 2013), 57–74.

4. Augustine, *City of God*, 8.5.

5. Augustine, *City of God*, 8.6.

6. Augustine, *City of God*, 8.6. See Marcia Colish, *The Stoic Tradition from Antiquity to the Early Middle Ages*, 2nd ed. (Leiden: Brill, 1990), 142–48.

other pagans, such as the Stoics, promoted the idea of common notions (*ennoiai*), which embraces logic, rational philosophy, and bodily senses, which are, again, things that all testify to the existence of God who has given them to humans.[7] But as much as Augustine praised pagan philosophers for the accuracy of their natural theology, he was also careful to point out its shortcomings. There is a difference between learning about God through the "elements of the world" rather than "according to God." Augustine invokes Paul's warning in Colossians 2:8 not to be deceived by philosophy and vain deceit. The Platonists and Stoics have a natural theology marked by errors.[8]

Nevertheless, Augustine seeks to explain how one like Plato could have perceived God's nature apart from Scripture. He entertains the possibility that Plato somehow came across the Old Testament, but in the end concludes that the specific source of his natural theology was immaterial given that he draws conclusions from the creation, or what he elsewhere calls the "book of nature."[9] Augustine, for example, writes, "Some people read books in order to find God. Yet there is a great book, the very appearance of created things. Look above you; look below you! Note it; read it! God, whom you wish to find, never wrote that book with ink. Instead, He set before your eyes the things that He had made."[10] Augustine promoted the liberal reading of the book of nature by looking for God's testimony in history, the human body, engineering arts, mathematics, and rhetoric. Christians need not fear the teaching of the philosophers but instead recognize that unbelievers possess the truth, even if unjustly. Christians, he argues, can take the truth that unbelievers have and put it to good use. But in the end, as Christians pursue the truth, they must do so through faith seeking understanding; that is, reason must be subordinated to faith, and faith must submit to the

---

7. Augustine, *City of God*, 8.7.

8. Augustine, *City of God*, 8.10.

9. Augustine, *City of God*, 8.11.

10. Augustine, *The Essential Augustine*, ed. Vernon J. Bourke (New York: New American Library, 1964), 123 (Bourke translates from sermon 126.6 in *Miscellanea Agostiniana*, ed. G. Morin [Rome: Vatican, 1930], 1:355–68); Hall, "Natural Theology in the Middle Ages," 59.

authority of God's revelation.[11] Much of what Augustine opined regarding natural theology continued in medieval theologians to varying degrees.

Anselm of Canterbury (1034–1109) is perhaps one of the best-known advocates of natural theology in the Middle Ages, as he famously continued in the Augustinian mold of *fides quarens intellectum*, or "faith seeking understanding."[12] Though unlike Augustine's *a posteriori* reading of the creation, Anselm promoted *a priori* arguments in his *Monologion* and *Proslogion*. In the *Monologion* Anselm avoids proofs that rest on Scripture, whereas the *Proslogion* arguably rests upon faith and the authority of Scripture, which reflects its genre as a prayer to God, literally, "words to another."[13] Anselm's argument falls within the pale of what constitutes natural theology, but not everyone has been convinced of its persuasiveness, most notably Thomas Aquinas (1225–1274).[14] Aquinas had a greater affinity for *a posteriori* arguments and believed that one could rationally demonstrate the existence of God because reason and revelation both proceed from God, and thus a valid argument from reason would never oppose Scripture.[15] Aquinas therefore advanced his five proofs for the existence of God, but these arguments were not a rationalist prolegomenon to his body of doctrine that he unfolds in his *Summa Theologica*.[16] Rather, Aquinas begins his *Summa* on the foundation of Scripture, and his five proofs function as a means

---

11. Hall, "Natural Theology in the Middle Ages," 59.

12. Anselm, *Proslogion*, trans. M. J. Charlesworth, in *The Major Works*, ed. Brian Davies and G. R. Evans (Oxford: Oxford University Press, 1998), 87.

13. Marilyn McCord Adams, "Praying the *Proslogion*: Anselm's Theological Method," in *The Rationality of Belief and the Plurality of Faith*, ed. Thomas D. Senor (Ithaca, N.Y.: Cornell University Press, 1995), 13–39; Gavin R. Ortlund, *Anselm's Pursuit of Joy: A Commentary* (Washington, D.C.: Catholic University of America Press, 2020).

14. Thomas Aquinas, *Summa Theologica* (repr., Allen, Tex.: Christian Classics, 1948), Ia, q. 2, art. 1, ad 2; Hall, "Natural Theology in the Middle Ages," 61.

15. Hall, "Natural Theology in the Middle Ages," 64.

16. Contra K. Scott Oliphint, *Thomas Aquinas* (Phillipsburg, N.J.: P&R, 2017); cf. Richard A. Muller, "Reading Aquinas from a Reformed Perspective: A Review Essay," *Calvin Theological Journal* 53, no. 2 (2018): 255–88; Paul Helm, "*Thomas Aquinas* by K. Scott Oliphint: A Review Article," *Journal of IRBS Theological Seminary* (2018): 169–93.

of confirming the legitimacy of the claims of Scripture.[17] In other words, the God of the Bible is also the God of creation, the external world to which Scripture points. Some have willfully misunderstood the role of Aquinas's proofs because they have read postmedieval versions of his arguments back into his *Summa*. Or, at best, the proofs only establish a generic theism rather than the existence of the God of the Bible. Critics seldom note, however, that in both his *Summa Theologica* and his *Summa Contra Gentiles*, Aquinas does not cease his arguments with the proofs but proceeds to unfold the whole body of Christian doctrine that culminates in Christ and eschatology.

After Aquinas natural theology was reshaped in the hands of John Duns Scotus (1265/6–1308) and William of Ockham (ca. 1287–1347). Scotus doubted that one could reliably argue from the creation back to the Creator. Scotus famously opined that we can no more conclude that God is wise from observing wisdom in creatures than we would have reason to believe that God is a stone.[18] Ockham believed that the idea of self-moving souls was a counterexample to the claim that whatever is moved is moved by another agent, thus the argument from motion is not self-evident.[19] The doubts of Scotus and Ockham about the profitability of natural theology were not shared by all, as late medieval theologian Raymond of Sabunde (ca. 1385–1436) reveals in his *Theologia Naturalis, sive Liber creaturarum* (Natural theology, or the book of creatures).[20] Sabunde follows the two-books theme of Augustine but expands upon it in his work. He argues that different creatures constitute the letters of the book of creation, which humans can read through their senses. The book of nature is open to all and cannot be destroyed, misinterpreted, or falsified, but the unbaptized are incapable of reading all of the book,

---

17. Richard A. Muller, "The Dogmatic Function of St. Thomas' 'Proofs': A Protestant Appreciation," *Fides et Historia* 24, no. 2 (1992): 15–29.

18. John Duns Scotus, *Philosophical Writings: A Selection*, trans. Allan Wolter (Indianapolis: Hackett, 1987), 25; Hall, "Natural Theology in the Middle Ages," 67.

19. Hall, "Natural Theology in the Middle Ages," 67.

20. Raymond of Sabunde, *Theologica Naturalis, sive Liber creaturarum specialiter de homine et de natura eius in quantum homo et de his que sunt ei necessaria ad cognoscendum seipsum et Deum et omne debitum ad quod homo tenetur et obligatum tam Deo quam primo* (n.p.: Martinus Flach, 1496).

and there are certain truths that surpass the powers of reason, thus there is some need of Scripture to overcome these deficiencies.[21] These broad trends within the patristic era and Middle Ages set the stage for the Reformation appropriation of natural theology.

Despite the claims of nineteenth- and twentieth-century theologians and historians, the Reformers did not scuttle natural theology.[22] Given the onset of the Renaissance, however, Reformation-era natural theology took on a different form, though maintaining a continuity with the earlier patristic and medieval patterns. Even though modern historians and theologians paint Calvin as one who rejected natural theology, the historical facts paint a different picture. Calvin believed that there were innumerable evidences that manifest the wisdom of God that even the most uneducated and ignorant persons could perceive.[23] But unlike the medieval arguments of Anselm and Aquinas, Calvin's natural theology bore the marks of Renaissance humanism. Calvin neither presents *a priori* arguments such as those that appear in Anselm's *Proslogion*, nor *a posteriori* arguments such as those in Aquinas's summae. Instead, he appeals to the arguments of Cicero (106–43 BC) in his *De Naturam Deorum* (On the nature of the gods).[24] Cicero's work captures common Stoic conceptions about natural theology that Calvin found agreeable to his own theology. In his work Cicero makes a number of claims about the gods, particularly the idea that they can be known through the

---

21. Hall, "Natural Theology in the Middle Ages," 68–70.

22. For treatments of the positive use of natural theology by the Reformers, see Michael Sudduth, *The Reformed Objection to Natural Theology* (London: Routledge, 2016); cf. Richard A. Muller, "Was It Really Viral? Natural Theology in the Early Modern Reformed Tradition," in *Crossing Traditions: Essays on the Reformation and Intellectual History in Honour of Irena Backus*, ed. Maria-Cristina Pitassi and Daniela Solfaroli Camillocci (Leiden: Brill, 2018), 507–31 (here 507–9); David VanDrunen, "Presbyterians, Philosophy, Natural Theology, and Apologetics," in *The Oxford Handbook of Presbyterianism*, ed. Gary Scott Smith and P. C. Kemeny (Oxford: Oxford University Press, 2019), 457–73 (here 458–61).

23. John Calvin, *Institutes of the Christian Religion*, trans. Henry Beveridge (Grand Rapids: Eerdmans, 1957), I.v.2.

24. Cicero, *De Naturam Deorum*, trans. H. Rackham, Loeb Classical Library (Cambridge, Mass.: Harvard University Press, 1972).

creation, an idea that Calvin appropriates in the opening five chapters of his *Institutes* and in his Romans commentary.[25]

Calvin states that when Paul argues that the gentiles do by nature what the law requires, the Greeks call this *prolepsis*, or "preconception."[26] He also speaks of fallen human beings possessing the seed of religion, a natural disposition to know God, the light of nature, and the readily apparent signs of divinity throughout the creation. Echoing Cicero, Calvin writes, "But, as a heathen tells us, there is no nation so barbarous, no race so brutish as not to be imbued with the conviction that there is a God."[27] Like Cicero, who appeals to the intricacy and marvels of the human body, Calvin claims this, too, is evidence for God's existence.[28] The idea appears in Aristotle (384–322 BC), among others, who called the human body a *microcosmos* that found its analog in the *cosmos*, though Calvin only makes reference to "philosophers."[29] In fact, Calvin does not actually begin to cite Scripture in his opening natural-theological arguments until the fourth chapter, a fact obscured by the McNeill and Battles edition of the *Institutes*, which inserts forty-three Scripture citations that do not appear in Calvin's opening five chapters.[30] Calvin does not begin his formal treatment of Scripture until book 2 of the *Institutes*.[31]

---

25. Egil Grislis, "Calvin's Use of Cicero in the Institutes I:1–5—A Case Study in Theological Method," *Archiv für Reformationsgeschichte* 62, no. 1 (1971): 5–37; Muller, "Was It Really Viral?," 511–13.

26. John Calvin, *The Epistles of Paul the Apostle to the Romans and to the Thessalonians*, trans. Ross Mackenzie, vol. 8 of *Calvin's New Testament Commentaries*, ed. T. F. Torrance and David F. Torrance (1960; repr., Grand Rapids: Eerdmans, 1996), comm. Rom. 2:14–15 (pp. 96–97).

27. Calvin, *Institutes* (1957), I.iii.1.

28. Calvin, *Institutes* (1957), I.v.2.

29. Calvin, *Institutes* (1957), I.v.3; cf. Aristotle, *Physics*, trans. Daniel Graham (Oxford: Clarendon, 1999), 8.2 (252b); George Perrigo Conger, *Theories of Macrocosms and Microcosms in the History of Philosophy* (New York: Columbia University Press, 1922).

30. Cf. John Calvin, *Institutio Religionis Christianae* (Geneva: Robert Stephanus, 1559); John Calvin, *Institutes of the Christian Religion*, ed. John T. McNeill, trans. Ford Lewis Battles (Philadelphia: Westminster, 1960), I.i–v.

31. Stephen Grabill, *Rediscovering the Natural Law in Reformed Theological Ethics* (Grand Rapids: Eerdmans, 2006), 82–83; Muller, "Was It Really Viral?," 520.

Calvin marshals all of this natural revelation to make the theological point that fallen human beings undoubtedly know of the existence of God. Thus, in concert with the earlier catholic tradition, Calvin maintains that the natural knowledge of God, and what may be discerned from it, are insufficient to give fallen humans a saving knowledge of God.[32] But Calvin does admit a natural theology of the regenerate when he states that one can rightly read the creation if one wears the corrective lenses of Scripture.[33] Notably, Calvin does not say that the Scriptures are the *eyes* but that they come to the aid of eyes weakened by sin.[34] In other words, natural theology is valid but only beneficial if used in concert with Scripture.

Calvin stands in the broader catholic tradition and particularly echoes Augustine and Sabunde regarding the idea of God's two books, nature and Scripture. Along with Theodore Beza (1519–1605) and Pierre Viret (1511–1571), Calvin penned the Gallican Confession (1559), which was adopted by the French church. They write in the confession: "God reveals himself to men; firstly, in his works, in their creation, as well as in their preservation and control. Secondly, and more clearly, in his Word, which was in the beginning revealed through oracles, and which was afterward committed to writing in the books which we call the Holy Scriptures" (art. 2).[35] Guido de Bres (1522–1567) built upon the Gallican Confession with his own Belgic Confession (1563) but makes explicit what lies implicit in the Gallican concerning the book of nature:

> We know God by two means: First, by the creation, preservation, and government of the universe, since that universe is before our eyes like a beautiful book in which all creatures, great and small, are as letters to make us ponder the invisible things of God: God's

---

32. Calvin, *Institutes* (1957), I.v.14.

33. Calvin, *Institutes* (1957), I.vi.1.

34. Abraham Kuyper, "The Natural Knowledge of God," trans. Harry Van Dyke, *Bavinck Review* 6 (2015): 73–112 (here 84).

35. Unless otherwise noted, quotations from confessional documents come from Jaroslav Pelikan and Valerie Hotchkiss, eds., *Creeds and Confessions of Faith in the Christian Tradition*, 3 vols. (New Haven, Conn.: Yale University Press, 2003).

> eternal power and divinity, as the apostle Paul says in Romans 1:20. All these things are enough to convict humans and to leave them without excuse. Second, God makes himself known to us more clearly by his holy and divine Word, as much as we need in this life, for God's glory and for our salvation. (Belgic Confession, art. 2)

This confessional codification demonstrates that Reformation era Reformed theologians shared a broad continuity on natural theology with earlier patristic and medieval theologians. Contrary to the claims of a number of modern theologians, Calvin does not depart from medieval or Renaissance epistemology (Frame), reject categories like natural law (Lang), deny that fallen humans can have true knowledge derived from the creation (Barth), make a complete break with scholastic theology and its conceptions of natural theology and ethics (Van Til), or begin with God's self-disclosure in Scripture (Dooyeweerd).[36] This is not to say, however, that Calvin and other Reformed theologians repristinated medieval arguments but that there is a continuity between them. Calvin and the Reformers do not, for example, talk about *theologia naturalis* (natural theology), but rather the knowledge of God available in creation. But there is also no outright rejection of natural theology despite many modern claims to the contrary.[37]

The use and explicit promotion of natural theology began in the period of early orthodoxy. One of the earliest examples comes from the work of Franciscus Junius (1545–1602) and his *Treatise on True*

---

36. John Frame, *A History of Western Philosophy and Theology* (Phillipsburg, N.J.: P&R, 2015), 174; August Lang, "Reformation and Natural Law," in *Calvin and the Reformation*, trans. J. Gresham Machen (New York: Revell, 1927), 56–98 (here 69, 72); Karl Barth, *Natural Theology: Comprising Nature and Grace by Professor Dr. Emil Brunner and the Reply No! by Dr. Karl Barth* (repr., Eugene, Ore.: Wipf & Stock, 2002), 94n88, 100–105, 107; Cornelius Van Til, *Defense of the Faith*, 3rd ed. (Phillipsburg, N.J.: Presbyterian and Reformed, 1966), 210; Van Til, *Common Grace and the Gospel* (Phillipsburg, N.J.: Presbyterian and Reformed, 1972), 93–94; Herman Dooyeweerd, *In the Twilight of Western Thought* (Grand Rapids: Paideia, 2012), 116; Dooyeweerd, *Reformation and Scholasticism in Philosophy*, vol. 1, *The Greek Prelude*, ed. D. F. M. Strauss, trans. Ray Togtmann, in *The Collected Works of Herman Dooyeweerd*, series A, vol. 5 (Grand Rapids: Paideia, 2012), 15.

37. Richard A. Muller, *Post-Reformation Reformed Dogmatics*, 2nd ed. (Grand Rapids: Baker Academic, 2003), 1:271; Muller, "Was It Really Viral?," 516–17, 525–28.

Theology.[38] In this work on theological prolegomena, Junius discusses the relationship between natural (revealed) theology and supernatural (also revealed) theology. The latter rests on the basis of the former. That is, according to Junius, nature and grace are the two forms for the communication of revealed theology.[39] Other early orthodox theologians contributed to the developing discussion of natural theology. One such theologian, Johann Heinrich Alsted (1588–1638), wrote his *Theologia Naturalis* in the context of developing a philosophical curriculum for Reformed academies and universities that included the study of metaphysics and natural theology.[40] The works of Junius and Alsted represent an expansion of the theology of the Reformation; the Reformers were largely interested in expounding supernatural theology in their works of catechetical, scholastic, or positive theology.[41] This does not mean, as some claim, that the Reformed theologians were tempted to make friends with the line of Cain and thus corrupt the biblical theology of the Reformation, which supposedly was free from all nonbiblical influences.[42] Rather,

38. Franciscus Junius, *A Treatise on True Theology: With the Life of Franciscus Junius*, trans. David C. Noe (Grand Rapids: Reformation Heritage Books, 2014); Junius, *De theologia vera* (Leiden: Ex Officina Plantiniana, 1594).

39. Willem van Asselt, introduction to *A Treatise on True Theology*, by Franciscus Junius, xl; also Van Asselt, "The Fundamental Meaning of Theology: Archetypal and Ecyptal Theology in Seventeenth-Century Reformed Thought," *Westminster Theological Journal* 64, no. 2 (2002): 319–35 (here 333). Nathan Shannon erroneously claims that Junius writes only of a postfall "hamartic natural theology," which is not true theology. See Nathan D. Shannon, "Junius and Van Til on Natural Knowledge of God," *Westminster Theological Journal* 82, no. 2 (2020): 279–300. The essay is an effort to enhance "the historical credentials" of Cornelius Van Til. But such claims fail to factor the structure of Junius's argument, namely, that revealed theology consists in two forms, natural and supernatural, both true; the former grounded on natural capacities of human beings, the latter on grace, a point that Van Asselt notes but Shannon misses. Contra Shannon, Junius does not argue that there is "no activity of the natural man which may properly be called 'theology'" (Shannon, "Junius and Van Til," 279). I am grateful to Richard Muller for pointing out this issue.

40. Johann Heinrich Alsted, *Theologica Naturalis* (Prostějov: Antonius Hummius, 1615).

41. Muller, *Post-Reformation Reformed Dogmatics*, 1:272.

42. Contra Cornelius Van Til, *Herman Dooyeweerd and Reformed Apologetics* (Philadelphia: Westminster Theological Seminary, 1972), 3:17.

this was an organic development as the needs of academic instruction grew with the creation of Reformed educational institutions.

In this context, theologians like Alsted argued that natural theology could have both a preparatory and apologetic function; it could lead to the higher truths of revealed theology or could be the basis for debate with nonbelievers.[43] But like the Reformers before him, Alsted rested his understanding of natural theology upon Scripture; in the preface of his work he cites Psalm 19:2–3; Romans 1:19–20; and Acts 14:17.[44] And in concert with the earlier tradition, he appeals to reason, experience, and the book of nature (*liber natura*). Reason is the internal *principium* that all human beings possess and is also called the light of nature (*lumen naturae*) or the light of reason (*lumen rationis*). Universal experience is the external *principium* which all human beings experience outside of themselves. And the book of nature is the world, which testifies to divine things, though Scripture is necessary for a right reading of this book.[45] But Scripture is a mixed *principium*, that is, Scripture testifies to things that are also in nature.[46] Alsted believed that the purpose of natural theology is twofold: (1) to render human beings inexcusable and (2) to prepare them for the school of grace. Once again, he rested these ideas on Scripture, namely, Romans 1:19–20.[47] Like Calvin before him, and in concert with the early church, Alsted appeals to Augustine, Maximus the Confessor (ca. 580–662), and Cicero. Echoing Aquinas, Alsted maintains that nature and grace are not in conflict.[48] Alsted employs these principles to develop proofs for the existence of God, to understand God's essential attributes, and to establish God as creator and governor of the world, as well as to discuss angels and spiritual entities, humans as a microcosm, and physical being in its different properties. This does not mean supernatural theology lies on a foundation of natural theology.

43. Muller, *Post-Reformation Reformed Dogmatics*, 1:273.

44. Alsted, *Theologia Naturalis*, preface, 3; also Muller, "Was It Really Viral?," 521–25.

45. Alsted, *Theologia Naturalis*, 2, 5.

46. Alsted, *Theologia Naturalis*, 7.

47. Alsted, *Theologia Naturalis*, 3.

48. Alsted, *Theologia Naturalis*, 4.

Rather, his work was ultimately designed to refute atheists, Epicureans, and sophists in his own day, as the subtitle to his work indicates.[49]

The same trends continue in the period of high orthodoxy in the theology of the Westminster Confession (1647). The Westminster Confession begins with its chapter on Scripture, but the opening line of the confession gives a tip of the hat to natural theology: "Although the light of nature, and the works of creation and providence do so far manifest the goodness, wisdom, and power of God, as to leave men unexcusable..." (1.1).[50] This statement echoes themes that appear in Calvin about the function of natural revelation. But the confession also spells out other positive functions for natural theology, such as ordering circumstances of worship (1.6), a means by which unbelievers might morally frame their lives (10.4), and an ethical guardrail for the exercise of Christian liberty (20.4), as well as a means by which all people know that God exists, has lordship over all, is good, does good unto all, "and is to be feared, loved, praised, called upon, trusted in, and served" (21.1).[51]

Some, such as Cornelius Van Til (1895–1987), argue that the confession presents a "distinctive doctrine of natural revelation." Van Til believes that the distinctive character of the confession's natural theology emerges clearly from "how intimately it is interwoven with the Confession's doctrine of Scripture."[52] "God's revelation in nature," writes Van Til, "together with God's revelation in Scripture, form God's one grand scheme of covenant revelation of himself to man."[53] Van Til's description of the confession is accurate in and of itself, but his characterization of it

49. Muller, *Post-Reformation Reformed Dogmatics*, 1:303.

50. *The Humble Advice of the Assembly of Divines Now by Authority of Parliament Sitting at Westminster* (London: Company of Stationers, 1647).

51. See J. V. Fesko and Guy M. Richard, "Natural Theology and the Westminster Confession of Faith," in *The Westminster Confession into the 21st Century: Essays in Remembrance of the 250th Anniversary of the Westminster Assembly*, ed. J. Ligon Duncan (Fearn, U.K.: Mentor, 2009), 3:223–66; Wallace W. Marshall, *Puritanism and Natural Theology* (Eugene, Ore.: Pickwick, 2016); VanDrunen, "Presbyterians, Philosophy, Natural Theology," 461–62.

52. Cornelius Van Til, "Nature and Scripture," in *The Infallible Word: A Symposium by the Members of the Faculty of Westminster Theological Seminary*, ed. N. B. Stonehouse and Paul Woolley, 2nd ed. (Phillipsburg, N.J.: P&R, 2002), 263–301 (here 263–64).

53. Van Til, "Nature and Scripture," 264.

as unique is inaccurate. The confession falls within the general patterns of patristic, medieval, and Reformation expressions, that is, in terms of God's two books, nature and Scripture. Aquinas, for example, in his commentary on Romans 1:19–20, writes, "God manifests something to man in two ways: first, by endowing him with an inner light through which he knows: *send out your light and your truth* (Ps. 43:3); second, by proposing external signs of his wisdom, namely, sensible creatures: *he poured her out*, namely, wisdom, *over all his works* (Sir. 1:9). Thus God manifested it to them either from within by endowing them with a light or from without by presenting visible creatures, in which, as in a book, the knowledge of God may be read."[54] Similar observations appear in the Westminster Assembly's comments on Romans 1:19–20 in their *Annotations*, a commentary on the whole Bible.[55] From the vantage point of Paul's letter to Rome, Aquinas spies out the creation and reads it in concert with Scripture, as does the confession. This does not mean there are no differences between them. For example, Aquinas cites Sirach, an apocryphal book, which the confession rejects. But the overall patterns of argumentation in the confession and Aquinas are parallel.

Francis Turretin (1623–1687) continues in this same path when he affirms a place for the instrumental use of philosophy in theology. Like Aquinas before him, he believes that "grace does not destroy nature, but makes it perfect. Nor does the supernatural revelation abrogate the natural, but makes it sure."[56] In Turretin's construction, natural and supernatural revelation work in concert, thus philosophy, what can be known by the light of nature, can "serve as a means of convincing the Gentiles and preparing them for the Christian faith." Turretin explicitly and approvingly cites Clement of Alexandria (ca. 150–215), for the idea that philosophy "prepares the way for the most royal doctrine."

---

54. Thomas Aquinas, *Commentary on the Letter of Saint Paul to the Romans*, trans. F. R. Larcher, ed. John Mortensen and Enrique Alarcón (Lander, Wyo.: Aquinas Institute for the Study of Sacred Doctrine, 2012), comm. Rom. 1:16–20, §116 (pp. 40–41).

55. *Annotations Upon All the Books of the Old and New Testament*, 3rd ed. (London: Evan Tyler, 1657), comm. Rom. 1:19–20.

56. Francis Turretin, *Institutes of Elenctic Theology*, trans. George Musgrave Giger, ed. James T. Dennison Jr., 3 vols. (Phillipsburg, N.J.: P&R, 1992–1997), 1.13.3.

In Turretin's judgment, Clement follows the apostle Paul's example in Acts 14 and 17. In addition to Turretin's characterization of philosophy as a preparation for the gospel, he echoes the two-books theme when he says that things known through nature function as a "twofold revelation." Beyond this, philosophy (or the light of nature) serves as a rational instrument of clarification both to distinguish between right and wrong and to prepare the mind for the engagement with higher sciences. Like Augustine and Calvin, Turretin argues that the light of nature includes common notions, the knowledge of right and wrong written on the conscience, as Paul attests in Romans 2:14–15.[57] In another quotation from Clement, Turretin warns, "Let philosophy submit to theology, as Hagar to Sarah, and suffer itself to be admonished and corrected; but if it will not be obedient, cast out the handmaid."[58] These same patterns and arguments appear in a number of other high orthodox Reformed theologians, but this all changed with the more rationalist theologies of late orthodoxy.[59]

Some late orthodox theologians became intertwined with Cartesianism, and others, such as Jean-Alphonse Turretin (1671–1737), the son of Francis Turretin, gave greater emphasis to the role and power of reason in theology. Jean-Alphonse continues the two-books theme common to Reformed theology, but unlike his father who gave a limited role to the light of nature, he expands the scope and powers of reason. Jean-Alphonse writes, "For natural religion is the foundation of revealed, which cannot be known and explained but by principles drawn from it—On the other hand natural Theology is republished, perfected and illustrated, by revealed."[60] Other Reformed theologians, such as Johann Friedrich Stapfer (1708–1775), argue that revealed theology assumes but cannot prove the existence of God, whereas natural theology with

57. Turretin, *Institutes*, 11.1.12–17.

58. Turretin, *Institutes*, 1.13.4–5.

59. Muller, *Post-Reformation Reformed Dogmatics*, 1:305.

60. Jean-Alphonse Turretin, *Dissertations on Natural Theology* (Belfast: James Magee, 1777), 1; cf. Martin I. Klauber, *Between Scholasticism and Pan-Protestantism: Jean-Alphonse Turretin and Enlightened Orthodoxy at the Academy of Geneva* (Selinsgrove, Pa.: Susquehanna University Press, 1996), 62–103.

its theistic arguments is the foundation upon which revealed theology rests.[61] Despite the similarity that such an idea has with statements in Francis Turretin, for example, this formulation is different than high orthodox constructions. This eighteenth-century shift marks the end of a Reformed orthodox understanding of natural theology, especially as it relates to the idea that Scripture is the sole *principum cognoscendi theologiae* with reason serving as an instrument or handmaiden. This development warrants two observations about key differences between high and late orthodox formulations. First, for the high orthodox, natural theology was ultimately a natural theology of the regenerate (*theologia naturalis regenitorum*), and because it is nonsaving, it cannot serve as a locus for theology. Second, natural theology exists only because of supernatural theology; it does not serve as its foundation or basis.[62] For high orthodox theologians, therefore, natural theology never attempts to draw supernatural revelation under the domain of natural reason.[63] This state of affairs sets the stage for the immediate nineteenth-century historical context for Vos's natural theology lectures.

Natural Theology in the Nineteenth Century

The nineteenth century contains a wide range of expressions of natural theology. There are a number of notable works, for example, that treat the topic, including entries by Henry Brougham (1778–1868), William Paley (1743–1805), J. L. Dagg (1794–1884), T. B. Gallaudet (1787–1851), Baden Powell (1796–1860), and John Tulloch (1823–86).[64] In the nineteenth century Paley's *Natural Theology*

---

61. E.g., Johann Friedrich Stapfer, *Institutiones Theologiae Polemicae Universiae* (Zürich: Heidegger, 1757), 1.1.30 (p. 8), 1.3.1–8 (pp. 67–207).

62. Muller, *Post-Reformation Reformed Dogmatics*, 1:306–8.

63. Muller, *Post-Reformation Reformed Dogmatics*, 1:309.

64. Henry Brougham, *A Discourse of Natural Theology Showing the Nature of the Evidence and the Advantages of the Study* (Brussels: Lewis Hauman, 1835); William Paley, *Natural Theology: or, Evidences of the Existence and Attributes of the Deity Collected form the Appearances of Nature* (New York: Sheldon, 1879); J. L. Dagg, *The Evidences of Christianity* (Macon, Ga.: J. W. Burke, 1869); T. B. Gallaudet, *The Youth's Book on Natural Theology* (Hartford, Conn.: Cooke, 1833); Gallaudet, *The Connexion of Natural and Divine Truth*

was popular and there were many imitators.[65] Paley's work opens with the famous watch illustration, namely, that if one was walking along a path and found a watch on the ground, a person would eventually conclude that there was a watchmaker and designer and that the watch did not naturally appear.[66] Paley sets forth the numerous arguments from the creation that demonstrate the existence of God and reveal His personality, natural attributes, unity, and goodness.[67] In Paley's estimation, the most persuasive arguments lie in human anatomy, which reveal the design and wisdom of the Creator. Paley's arguments lie in continuity with Calvin's invocation of Galen and the intricacy of the human body, evident by the numerous diagrams of ligaments, the eye, epiglottis, tendons in the wrist and instep, muscles of the hands and feet, and the heart.[68] But Paley's work never invokes Scripture, that is, he does not read the book of nature in concert with the spectacles of special revelation. This omission is deliberate on Paley's part, as he believes that all of nature would motivate one to seek more information about the God of creation and find it in Scripture. Paley thus distinguishes between natural theology (or reason) and revelation, namely, Scripture. "Nothing which [a person] has learned from Natural Theology," writes Paley, "will diminish his desire of farther instruction, or his disposition to receive it with humility and thankfulness. He wishes for light: he rejoices in light."[69] As an Anglican, Paley is representative of common natural-theological expressions in the wider church, but it is especially necessary to contextualize Vos within the framework of Princeton Seminary.

Charles Hodge (1797–1878) is, of course, one of the chief theological figures associated with Princeton Seminary and in many respects establishes a comparative benchmark in his many theological writings, but especially those related to natural theology. Hodge's commentary

(London: Parker, 1856); John Tulloch, *Theism: The Witness of Reason and Nature to an All-Wise and Beneficent Creator* (Edinburgh: Blackwood, 1854).

65. Matthew D. Eddy, "Nineteenth-Century Natural Theology," in *Oxford Handbook of Natural Theology*, 100–118 (esp. 110).

66. Paley, *Natural Theology*, 5, 11.

67. Paley, *Natural Theology*, 229–91.

68. Paley, *Natural Theology*, 292, 307–72.

69. Paley, *Natural Theology*, 296.

on Romans was one of his earliest works, first published in 1832.[70] In his analysis of Romans 1:19–20, Hodge argues that the knowledge that unbelievers suppress is revelation that arises from the external world, a knowledge that humans can apprehend because God has given human nature the capacity to understand it. According to Hodge, God's revelation is both in the creation and in humanity's constitution.[71] Hodge supports these claims not only from his immediate interaction with Romans 1:19–20, but also 2:14–15 and Acts 14:17.[72] When he draws doctrinal conclusions from his exegesis, Hodge notes that "natural religion" is an insufficient guide to salvation, which stands in contrast to Paley's more optimistic assessment of humanity's willingness to follow the path from natural to supernatural revelation.[73] Hodge's comments unsurprisingly stand in contrast to Paley's arguments given the difference in genre: an exegetical commentary versus a work on natural theology. But these same trends continue in Hodge's later theological writings when he treats natural theology.

In the opening pages of his *Systematic Theology*, Hodge presents a scriptural argument for natural theology. There is a sense in which his earlier Romans exegetical labors serve as the foundation for his later theological endeavors, evident in the opening line of his treatment: "The Scriptures clearly recognize the fact that the works of God reveal his being and attributes."[74] Hodge then invokes Psalm 19:1–4; 94:8–10; Acts 14:15–17; 17:24–29; and Romans 1:19–21. On the basis of Scripture, then, Hodge concludes that people can know of the being and attributes

70. Paul C. Gutjahr, *Charles Hodge: Guardian of American Orthodoxy* (Oxford: Oxford University Press, 2011), 144; also see VanDrunen, "Presbyterians, Philosophy, Natural Theology," 463–65.

71. Charles Hodge, *A Commentary on the Epistle to the Romans: Abridged by the Author, for the Use of Sunday-Schools and Bible Classes* (Philadelphia: Henry Perkins, 1836), 33. I was unable to locate a copy of the original 1832 edition. The cited 1836 edition is the same as the 1880 edition (see Charles Hodge, *A Commentary on the Epistle to the Romans: For the Use of Sunday-Schools and Bible Classes*, 19th ed. [New York: Robert Carter, 1880], 33–34, 40–41).

72. Hodge, *Romans* (1880), 34.

73. Hodge, *Romans* (1880), 40–41.

74. Charles Hodge, *Systematic Theology* (New York: Scribner, Armstrong, 1873), 1:24.

of God, and upon the foundation of natural revelation create a natural theology. In this vein he identifies key works on the topic including those by Christian Wolff (1679–1754), Peter Mark Roget (1779–1869), Thomas Chalmers (1780–1847), Joseph Butler (1692–1752), and Paley.[75] Hodge wanted his readers to know where the boundaries of natural theology were. He rejected the "extreme opinion" regarding natural theology that precluded the need for supernatural revelation; he rejects the teaching of the rationalists, who argued that nature was sufficient to lead fallen humans to salvation. Hodge defines the limits and powers of natural theology and the truths of reason solely on the authority of Scripture.[76]

Hodge elsewhere addresses principles of natural theology in theology proper where he discusses the innate knowledge of God. He asks whether the knowledge of God is innate to all human beings and answers in the affirmative: "If it be true that all men do believe there is a God, and that no man can possibly disbelieve his existence, then his existence is an intuitive truth." Moreover, such has been the opinion in all ages of the church according to Hodge; he cites Cicero, Tertullian (ca. 155–240), and Calvin.[77] Hodge's argument and appeal to these three authorities reveal his agreement and continuity with the earlier tradition, especially the early modern Reformed tradition, on the boundaries of natural theology. Hodge does not rest the idea of the innate knowledge of God upon the precedent of tradition alone but returns to Romans 1:19–21, 32 as proof that all humans know God. He also appeals to Romans 2:12–16, where Paul speaks of the gentiles doing *by nature* what the law requires.

---

75. Christian Wolff, *Theologica Naturalis Methodo Scientifica Pertractata* (Verona: Dionysius Ramazini, 1738); Peter Mark Roget, *Animal and Vegetable Physiology Considered with Reference to Natural Theology*, 2 vols., The Bridgewater Treatises 5 (London: William Pickering, 1834); Thomas Chalmers, *On the Power, Wisdom and Goodness of God as Manifested in the Adaptation of External Nature to the Moral and Intellectual Constitution of Man*, 2 vols., The Bridgewater Treatises 1 (London: William Pickering, 1834); Joseph Butler, *The Analogy of Religion, Natural and Revealed, to the Constitution and Course of Nature*, 3rd ed. (London: John and Paul Knapton, 1740).

76. Hodge, *Systematic Theology*, 1:25.

77. Hodge, *Systematic Theology*, 1:194; Cicero, *De Natura Deorum*, 1.17; Tertullian, *Testimonium Anima*; Calvin, *Institutes* (1957), I.iii.3.

In his Romans commentary, he succinctly explains, "The heathen are not to be judged by a revelation of which they never heard. But as they enjoy a revelation of the divine character in the works of creation, chp. 1:19–20, and of the rule of duty in their own hearts, vs. 14, 15, they are inexcusable. They can no more abide the test by which they are to be tried, than we can stand the application of the severer rule by which we are to be judged. Both classes, therefore, need a Savior."[78] If Hodge's view of natural theology is in any way representative of Old Princeton, then the seminary stands in continuity with early modern Reformed views and not the rationalist versions of late orthodoxy.

The same may be said of other Princetonians such as B. B. Warfield (1851–1921). Despite the fact that Van Til and others have accused Hodge and Warfield of rationalism because of their commitments to Scottish Common Sense Realism, both theologians ground their understanding of natural theology in Scripture and stand in continuity with the early modern Reformed tradition.[79] This is not to say that Hodge and Warfield repristinated the earlier tradition, but on the key points of the legitimacy of natural theology, its location in the broader creation and innately in humans, the noetic effects of sin, the inability of natural theology to be used for salvation, and its subordination to Scripture, they stand in continuity with the Reformation and Reformed orthodoxy. One should also note that Hodge and Warfield do not exhaust the Old Princeton tradition. As we will see below, other Princetonians contributed to Vos's understanding of natural theology.

But before delving into an analysis of Vos's lectures, a brief overview of the positions of Abraham Kuyper (1837–1920) and Herman Bavinck (1854–1921) will assist in painting Vos's nineteenth-century historical context. In Kuyper's day he saw a twofold problem as it relates to natural

78. Hodge, *Romans* (1880), 52.

79. See B. B. Warfield, "The Idea of Systematic Theology," *The Presbyterian and Reformed Review* 7, no. 26 (1896): 243–71; Warfield, "The Task and Method of Systematic Theology," *The American Journal of Theology* 14, no. 2 (1910): 192–205; cf. Paul Kjoss Helseth, *Right Reason and the Princeton Mind: An Unorthodox Proposal* (Phillipsburg, N.J.: P&R, 2010); Fred G. Zaspel, *The Theology of B. B. Warfield: A Systematic Summary* (Wheaton, Ill.: Crossway, 2010). Contra Van Til, *Defense of the Faith*, 264–65.

theology. On the one hand, modernists rejected supernatural knowledge and relied solely on the natural knowledge of God as entirely sufficient. On the other hand, the church responded to modernism by tending to argue that supernatural knowledge was the only means of knowing God. Modernists rejected Scripture and the church ignored the book of nature.[80] Kuyper notes that early modern Reformed theologians were not so imbalanced. As evidence of the two sources of the knowledge of God, he cites Calvin's ideas of the *sensus divinitatis* and *semen religionis* and the Belgic Confession's second article, which speaks of the books of nature and Scripture.[81] In Kuyper's judgment, the reason that many in the church turned away from natural theology was because theologians separated the natural and supernatural knowledge of God and thus created a purely rational natural theology.[82] Theologians were tempted to place natural theology alongside special theology (*theologia specialis*) and viewed it as a discipline in its own right, the means by which one established God's being, attributes, works, providence, moral law, and the final judgment. Even though special theology revealed much about sin and grace, the lion's share of the knowledge of God came through natural theology. "This furnished natural theology," writes Kuyper, "the occasion to unfold its wings ever more broadly; to expand itself and lessen the importance of special theology; until finally it succeeded in stepping forth as a monarch and in contesting all right of utterance to special theology."[83] Kuyper was opposed to such a bifurcation but at the same time neither was he disposed to retreating entirely to special revelation. Kuyper believed natural and supernatural theology were inseparable: "That special revelation (*revelatio specialis*) is not conceivable without the hypothesis of natural theology, is simply because *grace* never creates one single new reality."[84] Why was Kuyper positively disposed

80. Kuyper, "Natural Knowledge of God," 73; Richard A. Muller, "Kuyper and Bavinck on Natural Theology," *Bavinck Review* 10 (2019): 5–35 (here 8).

81. Kuyper, "Natural Knowledge of God," 73–74; cf. Calvin, *Institutes* (1957), I.iii.1, I.v.1.

82. Muller, "Kuyper and Bavinck," 11.

83. Abraham Kuyper, *Principles of Sacred Theology*, trans. J. Henrik de Vries (Grand Rapids: Eerdmans, 1963), 372–73.

84. Kuyper, *Principles of Sacred Theology*, 373 (italics in the original).

toward natural theology when the trend in the church was to seek refuge in the fortress of Scripture?

There are two chief reasons why Kuyper was inclined toward natural theology: (1) he agreed with the early modern Reformed tradition's understanding of natural theology, and (2) he was influenced by idealist monism. First, Kuyper saw elements of the nineteenth-century church standing at too great a distance from the teaching of the Reformation. Kuyper's own study of early modern Reformed theology undoubtedly contributed to his positive reception of it. Kuyper, for example, edited a volume of the select disputations of Gisbert Voetius (1589–1676), which begins with a disputation on the role of reason in matters of faith.[85] Kuyper was aware of the Reformed connections to Aquinas and had a nuanced reception of him. He believed that no theologian worth his salt should ignore him, but he also took issue with Thomas for believing that theology had reached its apex in the positive use of Greek philosophy. This criticism, however, better applies to neo-Thomism rather than to Thomas himself.[86] Second, Kuyper was eager about idealist monism, "the new *German philosophy*, from Kant to Schelling," and its "splendid enthusiasm for organic oneness."[87] In other words, Kuyper rejected the division of natural and supernatural knowledge, which he believed created an unnecessary dualism. Instead, his idealist monism drove him to conceive of natural and supernatural knowledge as an organic unity.[88]

Bavinck was in basic agreement with Kuyper and even had an affinity to the idealist organic monism motif, but he sought a different solution to the modernist rejection of the supernatural knowledge of God.[89] Bavinck wanted to counter the one-sidedness of modern thought and account for both the objective nature of external reality and the

85. Gisbert Voetius, *Selectarum Disputationum Fasciculus*, ed. Abraham Kuyper (Amsterdam: Adam Wormser, 1887), 1–9.

86. Muller, "Kuyper and Bavinck," 13.

87. Abraham Kuyper, *The Antithesis between Symbolism and Revelation: Lecture Delivered before the Historical Presbyterian Society in Philadelphia, Pa.* (Edinburgh: T&T Clark, 1899), 12 (italics in the original); Muller, "Kuyper and Bavinck," 16.

88. Muller, "Kuyper and Bavinck," 16.

89. Muller, "Kuyper and Bavinck," 20. For the organic motif in Bavinck, see James Eglinton, *Trinity and Organism* (London: Bloomsbury T&T Clark, 2012). Vos also

subjective inward life in his efforts to skirt any form of dualism. Like Kuyper, Bavinck opposed the modernist rejection of supernatural revelation. He also turned away from neo-Thomism because he believed it was rationalistic.[90] But at the same time he had an appreciation for Aquinas and shared a broadly Thomist epistemology where knowing truth is only possible if we begin with the idea that knowing and being correspond to each other and that all intellectual knowledge begins with sense perception.[91] Bavinck traced the lineage of his epistemology from Aquinas and through Reformed theologians such as Amandus Polanus (1561–1610).[92] Bavinck therefore had a positive understanding of natural theology and only saw problems when it was separated from supernatural theology.

Like Kuyper, Bavinck observes that the Reformation employed natural theology and the proofs for the existence of God, but from within the context of faith. Calvin's starting point was the *semen religionis*, which was a part of the incontrovertible signs and witnesses of God's majesty in every particle of the cosmos: the star-filled heavens, the human body, the soul, and the providential superintendence of all things. But problems arose when theologians began to take the road of rationalism. "Natural theology was initially an account, in the light of Scripture, of what Christians can know concerning God from creation," but "it soon became an exposition of what nonbelieving rational persons could learn from nature by the power of their own reasoning." Bavinck identifies Voetius as one who distinguished between the Reformation versus rationalistic approaches, but others such as René Descartes (1596–1650) did not. The proofs were separated from supernatural revelation, and in Bavinck's assessment the self-sufficiency of rationalistic natural theology

exhibits this tendency. Geerhardus Vos, "The Prospects of American Theology," trans. Ed M. van der Maas, *Kerux* 20, no. 1 (2005): 14–52 (here 23, 24, 27).

90. Muller, "Kuyper and Bavinck," 20–21.

91. Herman Bavinck, *Christian Worldview* (1913), trans. and ed. Nathaniel Gray Sutanto, James Eglinton, and Cory C. Brock (Wheaton, Ill.: Crossway, 2019), 38–39; Muller, "Kuyper and Bavinck," 22.

92. Muller, "Kuyper and Bavinck," 23–24.

survived until Immanuel Kant (1724–1804) subjected the proofs to devastating critique.[93]

Bavinck was familiar with the various arguments for the existence of God, including the cosmological, teleological, ontological, moral, universal consent, and historical-theological.[94] Bavinck believed that these arguments were not *proofs*, because they were not logical, mathematically compelling arguments; to present them as proofs robs them of their ethical and religious character. Bavinck notes that people do not need convincing of their own existence, because prior to any argumentation, people are fully convinced of their existence, the existence of the world around them, the laws of logic, and morality by means of the indelible impressions that all of these things make upon the human conscience. We accept our existence instinctively. The same is true about God's existence. The arguments for God's existence, therefore, introduce a greater distinctness and lucidity, but are by no means the final grounds upon which our belief in God rests: "The proofs, as proofs, are not the grounds but rather the products of faith."[95] Thus, Bavinck writes,

> There is not an atom of the universe in which [God's] everlasting power and deity are not clearly seen. Both from within and from without, God's witness speaks to us. God does not leave himself without a witness, either in nature or history, in heart or conscience, in life or lot. This witness of God is so powerful, accordingly, that almost no one denies its reality. All humans and peoples have heard something of the voice of the Lord. The consent of all peoples is confirmation of the fact that God does not leave himself without a witness; it is humanity's response to the voice of God.[96]

The proofs have a place within Bavinck's natural theology as they function in concert with supernatural revelation. They are not arguments, per se, "that strike the mind of unbelievers with compelling force, but

---

93. Herman Bavinck, *Reformed Dogmatics*, ed. John Bolt, trans. John Vriend (Grand Rapids: Baker Academic, 2004), 2:78–79.

94. Bavinck, *Reformed Dogmatics*, 2:81–89.

95. Bavinck, *Reformed Dogmatics*, 2:90.

96. Bavinck, *Reformed Dogmatics*, 2:90.

'signs and testimonies' that never fail to make an impression" on the minds of all people. Isolated and detached from each other, they can be attacked, and critics can refrain from acknowledging their conclusions. "But conceived as testimonies," writes Bavinck, "and proclaimed as the revelation of the God of whose existence every human is by nature—and prior to any reasoning or study—assured in the very depths of his or her soul, they are of no small value."[97] Kuyper's and Bavinck's positive appraisals of natural theology set the context to examine Vos's education and lectures.

Vos's Education

Vos was born on March 14, 1862, in the Netherlands, where he also grew up. He attended the Amsterdam gymnasium, graduating in the summer of 1881. His father received a pastoral call to serve as the minister of the Spring Street Christian Reformed church in Grand Rapids, Michigan, which led the Vos family to move from the Netherlands to the United States.[98] Upon his arrival in Grand Rapids, Vos enrolled in the Theological School. The school's curriculum included instruction in rhetoric, psychology, geography, logic, and history, as well as theological education in dogmatics, historical theology, hermeneutics, exegesis, church history, symbolics, and pastoral theology. But it became quickly apparent that Vos's learning excelled his peers, and thus he was appointed as a teaching assistant to Gerrit Egbert Boer (1832–1904), the school's teacher. Vos enrolled in the school in 1881 but received his diploma in 1882 after he passed exams in Hebrew, biblical history, natural theology, biblical geography, and introduction to religion. As a teaching assistant he was paid $300 a year, but he also continued to take classes in advanced theology from Boer. By the end of his second year, in May 1883, Vos was offered a

97. Bavinck, *Reformed Dogmatics*, 2:91.

98. I have drawn biographical information from Danny Olinger, *Geerhardus Vos: Reformed Biblical Theologian, Confessional Presbyterian* (Philadelphia: Reformed Forum, 2018); George Harinck, "Herman Bavinck and Geerhardus Vos," *Calvin Theological Journal* 45, no. 1 (2010): 10–31 (here 20–27); Harinck, "Geerhardus Vos as Introducer of Kuyper in America," in *The Dutch American Experience*, ed. Hans Krabbendam and Larry J. Wagenaar (Amsterdam: VU Uitgeveri, 2000), 242–61 (here 244–49).

permanent teaching position at the school, but he was instead interested in attending Princeton Theological Seminary.

At the age of twenty-one Vos enrolled at Princeton with advanced standing, which meant he began as a middler. Vos began classes in the fall of 1883, though his biographer says that little is known of Vos's days at Princeton. There are clues, however, from the Princeton catalogs regarding the different courses that Vos took. The 1883–1884 Princeton catalog lists a curriculum of four years of study, though Vos only took two years of classes and did not take the fourth year. During the first year, students would have taken introductions to the Old and New Testaments, Hebrew, exegesis of select epistles of Paul, biblical geography and history, comparative religion, the relationship between philosophy and science to Christianity, theism, theological encyclopedia, ecclesiastical theology, and courses in preaching.[99] Vos, of course, bypassed this first year of courses given that he was admitted with advanced standing. The second year consisted in the study of Hebrew, Poetical Books, and Historical Books, which would have been taught by William Henry Green (1824–1900); and New Testament, specifically the life of Jesus and the Gospels, taught by Caspar Wistar Hodge (1830–1891). In didactic theology, Vos sat for courses in theology proper and anthropology, taught by Archibald Alexander Hodge (1823–1886); he also took church history from James C. Moffat (1811–1890), and a course on the relationship of philosophy and science to Christianity, which was taught by Francis L. Patton (1843–1932). William M. Paxton (1824–1904) taught courses in church polity and preaching, which Vos took.[100] During his first year of study, the catalog indicates that Vos enrolled in special courses in Old Testament exegesis with Professor Green and New Testament exegesis with Professor C. W. Hodge.[101] During Vos's

99. For an explanation of the early curriculum at Princeton, see David B. Calhoun, *Princeton Seminary* (Edinburgh: Banner of Truth, 1994), 1:83–99.

100. *Catalogue of the Theological Seminary 1883–84, Princeton, New Jersey* (Philadelphia: Caxton, 1883), 13.

101. *Catalogue of the Theological Seminary 1883–84*, 10.

second year, he took elective study in biblical theology of the New Testament with C. W. Hodge and Old Testament exegesis with Green.[102]

While Vos's studies in Old and New Testament are naturally relevant for his future labors in biblical theology, it is particularly his studies with Francis Patton and his course in the relationship between philosophy, science, and Christianity that are of interest for Vos's lectures on natural theology. Vos passed examination in natural theology while he was at the Theological School in Grand Rapids, which means he had studied the subject earlier in his education. Given that the Theological School was in its infancy, however, little is known about what books Vos might have read as a part of his curriculum or his own personal study. But Vos was no neophyte when he arrived at Princeton. Nevertheless, anonymously transcribed lecture notes from Patton's 1883 course on the theistic conception of the universe reveal a web of topics and names that later appear in Vos's own lectures, including David Hume (1711–1776), Auguste Comte (1798–1857), Herbert Spencer (1820–1903), G. W. F. Hegel (1770–1831), Max Müller (1823–1900), F. W. J. Schelling (1775–1854), Anselm, Descartes, Kant, and others.[103] The parallels between Patton's and Vos's lectures reveal that Vos employed the views of his professor and claimed them as his own. There will be analysis of Vos's use of Patton below.

In addition to his broad-based theological education, Vos exhibited an interest in biblical studies, evidenced by his senior paper, "The Mosaic Origins of the Pentateuchal Codes," which so impressed his professor, William Green, that Green persuaded A. C. Armstrong and Son to publish it. Green wrote an introduction to the work, which focused on demonstrating the Mosaic authorship and unity of the Pentateuch over against the source-critical theory of Julius Wellhausen (1844–1918), among others.[104] Vos ventured to Europe where he enrolled at

---

102. *Catalogue of the Theological Seminary 1884–85, Princeton, New Jersey* (Princeton, N.J.: Princeton, 1884), 10.

103. Francis L. Patton, *Notes from Lectures on Theistic Conception of the Universe* (Princeton, N.J.: n.p., 1883).

104. Geerhardus Vos, *The Mosaic Origin of the Pentateuchal Codes* (New York: A. C. Armstrong, 1886); cf. Julius Wellhausen, *Prolegomena zur Geschichte Israels*, 6th ed.

the University of Berlin during the 1885–1886 academic year. Around this time Vos began to receive invitations to teach at different theological institutions. Columbia Theological Seminary in Decatur, Georgia, extended an offer to Vos as a provisional instructor, but Vos politely declined the invitation due to unstated differences of opinion with seminary leadership.[105] Vos also received an invitation from Kuyper to teach Old Testament at the Free University of Amsterdam. The Synod of the Christian Reformed Church in North America also reached out, as they were seeking to hire the next professor of exegetical and dogmatic studies for the Theological School in Grand Rapids. Vos was nominated and elected to this position, but he would first go to the University of Strasbourg for another year of study in Semitic languages. Vos wrote his dissertation in German, *Die Kämpfe und Streitigkeiten zwischen den Banū 'Umajja und den Banū Hāšim* (The conflicts and disputes between the sons of Ummayya and the sons of Hasim), which focused on the textual criticism of an Arabic manuscript that recorded a dispute between two thirteenth-century Islamic sects. Once he received his degree, he departed Europe on May 19, 1888, to begin his new professorship at the Theological School in Grand Rapids.

Background to Vos's Lectures

Vos was installed as professor of didactic and exegetical theology on September 4, 1888. He delivered his inaugural address entitled "The Prospects of American Theology," where he argued that God does not give exhaustive knowledge of heaven, earth, life, and death, but he nevertheless reveals knowledge that is certain.[106] Among the topics that Vos taught were ancient history, biblical geography and history, Hebrew, historical theology, history of religion, symbolics, hermeneutics, preaching,

(Berlin: Georg Reimer, 1905); Wellhausen, *Prolegomena to the History of Ancient Israel*, trans. J. Sutherland Black and Allan Menzies (Edinburgh: Adam & Charles Black, 1885).

105. Geerhardus Vos to J. B. Mack, Columbia Theological Seminary, Board of Directors, 13 July 1885, Columbia Theological Seminary Archives, Decatur, Georgia. I am grateful to Brian Hecker, archivist at Columbia Theological Seminary Library, for alerting me to and getting me a copy of this letter.

106. Vos, "Prospects of American Theology," 24.

dogmatics, and natural theology. Vos taught at least twenty-five hours per week. His lectures in dogmatics totaled 1,892 handwritten pages and were eventually typeset, mimeographed, and bound.[107] Vos's dogmatics are now published in English translation.[108] On September 2, 1891, Vos began his third year of teaching at the Theological School and was appointed rector. To commemorate his appointment, Vos delivered an inaugural address, "The Doctrine of the Covenant in Reformed Theology," which was mostly a historical overview of the doctrine of the covenants, but Vos also offered his own views at times.[109] The address is important because it reveals Vos's knowledge of and affinity for classical Reformed theology. In Vos's role as professor of didactic and exegetical theology, he was teaching outside of his preferred field of biblical studies. But he was nonetheless eager and willing to investigate historic Reformed sources. In fact, he wrote to Warfield to ask advice on sources for his address.[110] Vos labored at the Theological School, but controversy in the Christian Reformed Church over Vos's supralapsarian doctrine of predestination led him to consider other opportunities.

Vos's former professor, William Green, had been pursuing Vos and was trying to recruit him to return to Princeton. Vos went back and forth about whether he should remain in Grand Rapids or make the move to Princeton. Vos eventually decided to accept the call from Princeton, and he began teaching in the newly created chair of biblical theology in the fall of 1893. Vos was formally installed and delivered his inaugural address on May 8, 1894, entitled "The Idea of Biblical Theology as a

107. Geerhardus Vos, *Dogmatiek van G. Vos, Ph.D. D.D.*, 5 vols. (Grand Rapids: n.p., 1910).

108. Geerhardus Vos, *Reformed Dogmatics*, trans. and ed. Richard B. Gaffin Jr. et al., 5 vols. (Bellingham, Wash.: Lexham, 2012–2016).

109. Geerhardus Vos, "The Doctrine of the Covenant in Reformed Theology," in *Redemptive History and Biblical Interpretation: The Shorter Writings of Geerhardus Vos*, ed. Richard B. Gaffin Jr. (Phillipsburg, N.J.: Presbyterian and Reformed, 1980), 234–70.

110. Geerhardus Vos to B. B. Warfield, 7 July 1891, in *The Letters of Geerhardus Vos*, ed. James T. Dennison Jr. (Phillipsburg, N.J.: P&R, 2005), 160–64 (hereafter: *Letters*).

Science and Theological Discipline."[111] Vos's appointment to the chair of biblical theology at Princeton marks a watershed in his career. His appointment was the beginning of a new chapter in his theological labors where he turned his attention almost exclusively to the discipline of biblical theology. Vos would no longer lecture on dogmatic or natural theology.

Methodology

Theological education has changed over the last century, and evidence of this appears in Vos's lecture methodology. Unlike Hodge's *Systematic Theology*, which reads like a regular book with chapters and paragraphs, Vos's lectures in dogmatics are in a question-and-answer format. This same style marks Vos's natural theology lectures. Vos begins his lectures by asking, "Where does natural theology correspond with revealed theology, and where is it distinguished from the latter?" This is the first of 224 questions and answers. While this lecture style might be unfamiliar to theological students today, it was common in the nineteenth century. The *dictaten* format means that the professor would read the questions and answers, and students would record the information in their notes. This is the lecture style, for example, for Kuyper's six-volume *college-dictaat* dogmatics.[112] The *dictaten* format of Vos's lectures also explains the dating of the manuscripts. There are three handwritten manuscripts: W. de Groot (April 13, 1895), L. J. Veltkamp (September 27, 1898), and a third, anonymous, incomplete, and undated set. The fact that both sets of dated notes originate from at least two or more years after Vos left the Theological School means that it is likely either that another professor dictated Vos's lectures to students after his departure—perhaps Gerrit Boer, Gerrit Hemkes (1838–1920), or Henricus Beuker (1834–1900)—or that one or another of these professors recommended study of Vos's manuscript. As Albert Gootjes indicates in his preface, the Veltkamp manuscript (and perhaps the De Groot manu-

111. Geerhardus Vos, *Inauguration of the Rev. Geerhardus Vos, PhD., D.D., as Professor of Biblical Theology* (New York: Anson D. F. Randolph, 1894).

112. See, e.g., Abraham Kuyper, *Locus De Creatione: College-dictaat van onderscheidene studenten* (Amsterdam: J. A. Wormser, 1891).

script) has the appearance of a clean copy made from an earlier draft, whereas the anonymous manuscript has the appearance of notes taken during a lecture. All three professors lectured in dogmatic theology between 1893 and 1898. So, even though Vos had departed, he still continued to influence theological training in Grand Rapids through the use of his notes on natural theology, either by colleagues who dictated them or by students who made copies and circulated them among themselves.

Sources

Given the nature of Vos's work as classroom lectures, he does not cite sources as he would in a published journal article or book. To a certain extent, his lectures parallel his dogmatics lectures, where there are no formal footnotes or citations. At the same time, in contrast to his dogmatics lectures, his natural theology lectures do substantively interact with a number of key figures and works by name and title. As he rehearses the history of natural theology, Vos, for example, begins in the patristic period with Augustine and John of Damascus (d. 749), continues through the Middle Ages with pseudo-Dionysius the Areopagite (fl. 6th cent.), Anselm, Abelard, Durandus of Saint-Pourçain (1275–1334), Raymond of Sabunde, and through to the Reformation (QQ. 17–28). As he traces its reception, he mentions post-Reformation works such as Alsted's *Theologia Naturalis* and the reception by Descartes and Wolff (QQ. 29–34). When he delves into the Enlightenment, he mentions numerous works, such as those by Kant (Q. 34). When he arrives at nineteenth-century works, he mentions the works of Paley and Otto Zöckler (1833–1906) (QQ. 37–39). Vos engaged a broad sweep of sources and figures, but the key question is, Which of these sources did Vos directly read? In other words, how much of Vos's lectures rely on primary sources versus secondary sources? To pose the question is not to doubt the quality of Vos's lectures, as all professors employ secondary literature. Rather, the query drives at the issue of what sources were formative for his views. To what degree do his lectures reflect his own analysis based on primary source texts versus relying upon the analysis of others?

As noted above, clusters of names that appear in Vos's lectures suggest that he gleaned material from his Princeton apologetics professor,

Francis Patton. In his lectures on theism, Patton discusses the genesis of theism, and he begins with Hume and then treats Comte, Spencer, Müller, and Schelling.[113] Vos treats the same series of names in his own lectures when he discusses the origins of the general concept of God. He traces the same line of thinkers from Hume, Comte, Spencer, and Müller, though he does not mention Schelling at this point (Q. 77). Vos is not mindless in his reliance on Patton, but he does largely repeat the same thoughts. Patton and Vos, for example, write:

Patton

Polytheism, according to H[ume], is prior to Monotheism. The advance out of the one into the other is not due to philosophic reflection and a growing appreciation of the unity of nature, but is explained by the tendency to flatter a local deity, to impute greatness, and so by degrees to invest him with the attribute of infinity. A view lacking every element of plausibility, and speculatively worthless.[114]

Vos

According to him [Hume], there first were many gods, and polytheism ruled the day. Through accidental, largely local circumstances one God then came to be venerated more than the others, until the others receded into the background and only a single one remained. This is how monotheism arose. This theory condemns itself, since it must take refuge in something accidental for its explanation (Q. 77.1).

The paragraphs are not identical, as the variation may be attributable to several factors: (a) Vos may have paraphrased Patton, (b) the lecturer may have paraphrased Vos's original manuscript, (c) the student may have paraphrased the lecturer, or (d) there was a combination of two or more of these different factors. But the point remains that Vos substantively echoes Patton.

113. Francis L. Patton, *Syllabus of Prof. Patton's Lectures on Theism* (Princeton, N.J.: Princeton, 1888), 3–4. Note: the title page indicates that the syllabus was "Printed, Not Published."

114. Patton, *Theism*, 3.

Vos's reliance upon Patton is evident throughout the section on theism. Patton's and Vos's statements about Comte are very similar:

Patton	**Vos**
The theory under notice is credited to Compte [*sic*], not because he is the originator of the term fetich [*sic*], nor yet because he has given the best account of fetischistic religions—for this distinction is due to F. Schultze, (Feitchismus)—because Compte first presented in reasoned form the doctrine that all religion begins in Fetichism and passes thence through Polytheism to Monotheism. Discussing the fetich-theory of religion (1) inquire into the origin and meaning of the word fetich, and (2) consider reasons for and against this view. Account of the word given in Max Müller's Hibbert Lectures, p. 54. Introduced by De Bross, 1760. Origin of the word found in the custom of Portuguese navigators, who called the inanimate objects worshipped by the people of West Africa—*feticos*.[115]	Comte's theory, also called "fetishistic"—not because he coined the name "fetish," but because he first defended the theory that all religion originated in or began with fetishism. The name "fetish" was first used by the French author De Brosses in 1760. Portuguese seafarers saw the indigenous peoples on the coast of Africa venerate such objects as their amulets or rosaries, and gave this religion the name *fetices*, since they gave their sacred objects the Portuguese name *fetiço* (magic). (Q. 77.2)

Patton and Vos proceed in their lectures to explain the nature of a fetish, and even mention many of the same concepts. Their respective analyses are not exact copies, but there are enough conceptual similarities to suggest that Vos relied on Patton's lecture notes. Given that Vos was granted

115. Patton, *Theism*, 4.

advanced standing, he likely did not take Patton's class on theism, as it was a first-year course.[116] Vos therefore likely accessed the 1888 printed edition of Patton's lectures.

There is further evidence that shows the connections between Vos and his apologetics professor. Patton lectured on antitheistic theories during his professorship at Princeton in which he treats pantheism. There are some similarities between Patton's and Vos's treatments of pantheism but not necessarily enough evidence to confirm that Vos accessed Patton's syllabus. Patton, for example, goes into great detail regarding the views of Baruch Spinoza (1632–1677) and supplies quotations from him.[117] Vos, on the other hand, only briefly mentions Spinoza (Q. 51.2). Patton references Jonathan Edwards (1703–1758) and his doctrine of continuous creation, which Patton states is not pantheistic; Edwards does not appear in Vos's treatment.[118] There are, however, some continuities, as both Patton and Vos discuss material and idealistic pantheism (Q. 48).[119] But beyond this modest similarity, the fact that Vos lectured on pantheism at least reveals a conceptual continuity between Vos and his former professor.

Another point of similarity between Vos and Patton emerges in their reference to other shared sources. In his *Summary of Doctrine*, Patton refers to the teleological argument in Charles Hodge's *Systematic Theology*, to the "numerous works on natural theology and to the volumes of lectures published by the Christian Evidence Society of London." Patton also mentions the work of Paley.[120] Patton's work was published in 1901, well after Vos left the Theological School. Nevertheless, Vos mentions Paley's *Natural Theology* and the "Bridgewater treatises" (Q. 37)

---

116. *Catalogue of the Theological Seminary 1884–85*, 13.

117. Francis L. Patton, *Syllabus of Prof. Patton's Lectures on the Anti-Theistic Theories* ([Princeton, N.J.: Princeton], n.d.), 9, 13, 14–17. The stamp on the interior of the document reveals that it entered the Princeton library collection in 1910, which would have been well after Vos departed the Theological School and was teaching at Princeton Seminary.

118. Patton, *Anti-Theistic Theories*, 4.

119. Patton, *Anti-Theistic Theories*, 12–13.

120. Francis L. Patton, *A Summary of Christian Doctrine* (Philadelphia: Westminster, 1901), 13; cf. Hodge, *Systematic Theology*, 1:24.

and Christian Wolff (Q. 33), which are the same sources that Hodge references in his discussion of natural theology in his *Systematic Theology*.[121] The fact that Vos and Patton both cite these works shows that, at a minimum, they operate within the matrix of the sources and discussions of Princeton. Maximally, Hodge informed the views of Patton and Vos. These observations only begin to scratch the surface of Vos's sources, but they at least show the organic connections between Vos and Old Princeton. Despite the fact that he was only at Princeton for two years, he nevertheless carried and employed his education with him in his later teaching career at the Theological School.

Another potentially important pool of sources lies in the works and correspondence between Vos, Kuyper, Bavinck, and Warfield. In the published letters of Vos there are thirty-two letters dated from 1883 until July 1893, just several months before Vos moved to Princeton to assume the chair of biblical theology. Of these thirty-two letters, there are ten letters to Kuyper, six to Bavinck, and fourteen to Warfield.[122] As a student, and later as a professor at the Theological School, Vos was in regular dialogue with these three theologians, not to mention Vos's time at Princeton as a student when he directly interacted with Warfield. Many of these letters are pedestrian in nature, as they recount details about reviews, translations, and coordinating efforts to solicit contributions from Kuyper and Bavinck for the *Princeton Theological Review*. But there are occasional hints of streams of influence among the correspondents. In an 1886 letter to Kuyper, for example, Vos writes, "Directly and indirectly your book has exerted a formative influence on me."[123] What work Vos has in mind is unclear. In an 1887 letter to Bavinck, Vos recounts the lectures of his professor, Theodor Nöldeke (1836–1930) on Kant's *Critique of Judgment*, which informed Vos's analysis of Kant in his lectures. He also mentions Henri du Marchie van Voorthuizen (1824–1894) on Kant's *Critique of Pure Reason*.[124] But in

121. Hodge, *Systematic Theology*, 1:24.

122. *Letters*, 7–8.

123. Vos to Abraham Kuyper, 28 May 1886, in *Letters*, 116.

124. Vos to Herman Bavinck, 17 June 1887, in *Letters*, 126; Henri du Marchie van Voorthuizen, *De Theorie der Kennis van Immanuel Kant* (Arnhem, Netherlands: n.p., 1886).

a revealing 1889 letter to Warfield, Vos mentions Kuyper's *Encyclopedia*; this is significant because it is a letter written two years into Vos's professorship at the Theological School. Vos laments to Warfield that theological encyclopedia was not taught in seminaries as a regular topic. And then Vos reminisces, "I remember very well however, during my Seminary days at Princeton, to have heard Prof. Patton speak with great enthusiasm of the difficulties and attractions alike of such a work as Dr. Kuyper has undertaken."[125] This comment reveals that Patton's ideas on theological encyclopedia were cemented in Vos's mind, which explains the similarities between Vos, Patton, and Warfield on the nature, function, and place of natural theology within the encyclopedia.

The letters also disclose that Vos stayed abreast of theological developments through reading the *Presbyterian Review, Presbyterian and Reformed Review, Theologisch Tijdschrift*, various theological works, and Dutch newspapers. Vos was receiving regular shipments of books from the Netherlands and asked to be billed biannually or annually.[126] In addition to this, Vos conveys the plans to translate Bavinck's article on recent dogmatic thought in the Netherlands.[127] In an 1891 letter to Kuyper, Vos interacts with him on matters related to Kuyper's supralapsarianism and invokes a catena of sources that reveal Vos was well-read in early modern Reformed theology, including the *Leiden Synopsis*, the fathers of Dordt (Gomarus, Bogermann, Voetius, Maccovius), and Calvin.[128] One of the most significant letters comes from 1891 when Vos wrote to Warfield about covenant theology. In this letter Vos reveals that

Another potential source might be the dissertation of C. W. Hodge Jr., though this was published the year after Vos started his post at Princeton. The dissertation might reveal, however, that Vos gleaned ideas from Hodge through personal interaction. See C. Wistar Hodge Jr., *The Kantian Epistemology and Theism: A Dissertation Presented to the Faculty of Princeton College for the Degree of Doctor of Philosophy* (Philadelphia: MacCalla, 1894).

125. Vos to Warfield, 22 October 1889, in *Letters*, 129–30. Vos comments about this deficiency in his inaugural address. Vos, "Prospects of American Theology," 27; see also Harinck, "Bavinck and Vos," 23–24.

126. *Letters*, 131–32, 136–37.

127. Vos to Warfield, 5 August 1890, in *Letters*, 143; Herman Bavinck, "Recent Dogmatic Thought in the Netherlands," trans. Geerhardus Vos, *Presbyterian and Reformed Review* 3, no. 10 (1892): 209–28.

128. Vos to Kuyper, 21 February 1891, in *Letters*, 148–51.

his views on the covenant are those of the "Westminster Catechism" and Petrus van Mastricht (1630–1706), but Vos did not advocate the *pactum salutis* and consequently came under crushing criticism. In this letter Vos asks Warfield for help in identifying early modern Reformed sources for his research on the topic and in preparation for his lecture on the history of the covenant in the Reformed tradition.[129]

These thirty-two letters do not present definitive clues regarding the sources of Vos's natural theology lectures, but they uncover the fact that Vos was very much in line with his Princeton professors, such as Patton. They also show that the general dialogue between Vos, Kuyper, Bavinck, and Warfield was undoubtedly formative upon him.[130] There is unquestionably more spadework to be done to unearth the sources that lie behind Vos's lectures, but establishing his connections to Princeton faculty and views on natural theology assist in contextualizing Vos's views.

Relationship to Reformation and Post-Reformation Views

Beyond the question of sources, how do Vos's lectures compare with early modern Reformed and later nineteenth-century Reformed thought on natural theology? Does Vos agree with the Reformers, Kuyper, and Bavinck, or do his lectures stand closer to Paley's *Natural Theology*? By and large, Vos's lectures are in agreement with the Reformers and the views of Kuyper, Bavinck, and Old Princeton. The detailed answer to this question, however, requires greater nuance. The continuities and discontinuities between Vos and the broader Reformed tradition appear in (1) the place and function of natural theology, and (2) Vos's historical assessment of the tradition.

The Place and Function of Natural Theology according to Vos

First, as the above survey explains, Calvin saw natural theology rising out of Scripture not from the human's raw capacity to reason his or her

129. Vos to Warfield, 7 July 1891, in *Letters*, 160–64; Vos, "The Doctrine of the Covenant in Reformed Theology," 234–70.

130. Harinck, "Bavinck and Vos," 24.

way to God. Vos defines natural theology as "a knowledge of God that takes its content and method from the world as it presents itself to us as governed by fixed laws" (Q. 7). Vos then distinguishes between natural and revealed theology. Revealed theology is that which comes to humans as new and unusual, apart from nature, whereas natural theology comes purely from nature (Q. 8). Vos therefore contrasts *revelation* and *nature,* though this distinction might at first be misleading. To distinguish between these two ideas might give the impression that nature is not revelation, but this is not the case. Rather, Vos argues that revelation in the "wide" sense includes everything that God communicates to humans about Himself, including nature.[131] So, there is a sense in which nature is revelation. Instead of this broader definition, Vos distinguishes between revelation and nature so he can account for the special and direct way that God reveals Himself that does not appear in nature. Vos does not employ the terms, but his concern is semantic rather than substantive and echoes the concepts of general and special revelation.[132]

When Vos moves to anchor the idea of natural theology, he goes first to Scripture, not to reason. He cites Psalm 19:1–4; 94:8–10; Acts 14:15–17; 17:24–29; and Romans 1:19–21 (Q. 10).[133] These are the same passages of Scripture that Hodge cites in his treatment of natural theology; Vos lists these passages in the same order as Hodge.[134] This may mean that Vos referred to Hodge's treatment of the topic to write his own lectures. Moreover, like Hodge, Kuyper, Bavinck, and the early modern tradition, Vos states that natural theology is insufficient for salvation (Q. 11).[135] But further continuities arise with the role that he assigns to natural theology. Like the earlier tradition, Vos understands natural revelation to be sufficiently clear to hold people accountable concerning the need to worship and believe in God, "so that

---

131. Similarly, Bavinck, "Recent Dogmatic Thought," 215–16.

132. Cf. Geerhardus Vos, *Biblical Theology: Old and New Testaments* (Edinburgh: Banner of Truth, 2014), 19–23.

133. Note Vos's comments on the idea of peering out into creation from the vantage point of Scripture. Vos, "Prospects of American Theology," 23.

134. Hodge, *Systematic Theology*, 1:24–25.

135. Hodge, *Systematic Theology*, 1:25–26; see also Vos, "Prospects of American Theology," 21, 46.

they are without excuse" (QQ. 10, 12.1). Positively, natural theology is useful because it discretely teaches things that Scripture does not teach, though it assumes those things (Q. 12.2). It teaches people "to adore the wisdom of God" (Q. 12.3), and it is of use in apologetics to refute "those who have rejected the supernatural revelation of God" (Q. 12.4). These points show that Vos was in line with early modern Reformed views on natural theology, especially the views of Alsted. Recall, Alsted argued that natural theology was useful in refuting atheists and Epicureans.[136]

One of the more interesting statements that Vos makes comes in his explanation of the relationship between natural theology and metaphysics. In context, Vos equates metaphysics with philosophy, specifically the subjects of being (existence) and causality. In his understanding, Vos places natural theology between philosophy and theology (Q. 13). This reflects ideas later famously expressed by Warfield and common to Princeton, namely, that apologetics establishes the categories of theology: theism and then Christian theism. In an essay on the theological encyclopedia, Patton for example explained that natural theology was part of the department of philosophical theology. Moreover, "Natural Theology is the basis of Revealed Theology, and the true order of thought is found in the Saviour's words: 'Ye believe in God: believe also in me.'"[137] Noteworthy is that Kuyper makes the same point: "*Without the basis* of *natural* theology there is no *special* theology."[138] At first glance, Vos, Patton, and Kuyper might give the impression that they advocate a late orthodox understanding of natural theology, one where theologians first establish the principles of theism by reason and then transition to special revelation. While some have characterized Princeton's stance on apologetics in this fashion, the truth is quite different.

Warfield explains the overall approach and placement of apologetics in the following manner:

136. Bavinck makes a similar point in the essay that Vos translated; see Bavinck, "Recent Dogmatic Thought," 213.

137. Francis L. Patton, "Theological Encyclopaedia," *Princeton Theological Review* 2, no. 1 (1904): 110–36 (here 115).

138. Kuyper, *Principles of Sacred Theology*, 374 (italics in the original).

> But certainly, before we draw it [systematic theology], we must assure ourselves that there is a knowledge of God in the Scriptures. And, before we do that, we must assure ourselves that there is a knowledge of God in the world. And, before we do that, we must assure ourselves that a knowledge of God is possible for man. And, before we do that, we must assure ourselves that there is a God to know. Thus, we inevitably work back to first principles. And, in working thus back to first principles, we exhibit the indispensability of an 'Apologetical Theology,' which of necessity holds the place of the first among the five essential theological disciplines.[139]

Taken by itself, this lone statement might lend credence to the criticism that Warfield can only produce a general theism, but not the Christian theism of the Bible. Warfield anticipated this objection and argued that there were two important concomitants to apologetics. First, no one was ever converted to Christianity by apologetics: "We are not absurdly arguing that Apologetics has in itself the power to make a man a Christian or to conquer the world to Christ."[140] Only the Spirit's gift of faith enables a person to believe in Christ, but faith in Christ is rational, not irrational—it is not a "faith without grounds in right reason."[141] Note, Warfield does not say *reason* but *right* reason, that is, reason bridled by the Spirit through regeneration.[142] Warfield and the Princetonians were not advocating rationalism as some allege but only a robust scriptural notion of the powers of right reason to know God.

Second, it was never Warfield's intention to use apologetics merely to establish a generic theism. Apologetics was not interested in a minimal account of Christianity. The function of apologetics "is not to vindicate for us the least that we can get along with, and yet manage to call ourselves Christians; but to validate the Christian 'view of the world,'

139. B. B. Warfield, introduction to *Apologetics: or the Rational Vindication of Christianity*, by Francis R. Beattie (Richmond, Va.: Presbyterian Committee of Publication, 1903), 1:19–32 (here 24).

140. Warfield, introduction to *Apologetics*, 25.

141. Warfield, introduction to *Apologetics*, 25.

142. Helseth, *Right Reason*, 3–140; also Paul Kjoss Helseth, "'Congeniality' of Mind at Old Princeton Seminary: Warfieldians and Kuyperians Reconsidered," *Westminster Theological Journal* 77, no. 1 (2015): 1–14.

with all that is contained in the Christian 'view of the world,' for the science of men." Thus, "the function of Apologetics is not performed until it has placed in our hands God, Religion, Christianity and the Bible, and said to us, Now go on and explicate these fundamental facts in all their contents."[143] The overall methodology at work stands in line with the Reformation idea of God's two books: nature and Scripture. Warfield and the Princetonians believed that apologetics was supposed to establish objective evidence that all normally functioning minds throughout every age could consider, that which embodied the entire concrete knowledge of God accessible to humans.[144] This apologetic methodology stood in opposition to Ritschlian and Kuyperian understandings of apologetics.

Warfield was opposed to the rationalistic tendencies promoted by Albrecht Ritschl (1822–1889). Ritschl erected a wall between religious and theoretical knowledge.[145] Religion was only supposed to seek and find expression in value judgments, which were the product of the subjective human soul in its struggle for freedom. This subjective struggle stands opposed to theoretical knowledge, for which there is no place for a defense of the Christian faith to reason, and thus no need for apologetics. A parallel tendency to Ritschl's rationalism was mysticism, which eschewed apologetics in favor of the *testimonium Spiritus Sancti*, "the testimony of the Holy Spirit."[146] Warfield also critiqued Kuyper for his placement of apologetics. Despite the fact that he and Kuyper largely agreed on the function of natural theology, they nevertheless diverged on the place of apologetics. Warfield was effusive regarding Kuyper's status as a theological titan but bemoaned the fact that Kuyper relegated apologetics to a subset of systematic theology.[147] In fact, Kuyper only

143. Warfield, introduction to *Apologetics*, 31.

144. Warfield, introduction to *Apologetics*, 31–32.

145. Cf. Albrecht Ritschl, "Theology and Metaphysics," in *Three Essays*, trans. Philip Hefner (Philadelphia: Fortress, 1972), 151–217 (here 153, 154, 158, 160, 210); Herman Bavinck, "The Theology of Albrecht Ritschl," trans. John Bolt, *Bavinck Review* 3 (2012): 123–63 (here 133, 140, 144, 159).

146. Warfield, introduction to *Apologetics*, 20; see also Bavinck, "Recent Dogmatic Thought," 211.

147. Warfield, introduction to *Apologetics*, 21.

devotes some ten pages to apologetics in the third volume of his *Encyclopedia*.[148] Despite the collegiality and high esteem Warfield and Kuyper shared for each other, the two theologians would inadvertently create two competing schools of apologetic thought in the twentieth century. More will be said about this below.

All signs in his natural theology lectures point to the fact that Vos was in agreement with Hodge, Warfield, and Patton on the place and function of natural theology and apologetics.[149] In fact, confirmation of this conclusion comes from two different places in Vos's broader corpus. In his lectures on dogmatics, which were delivered around the same time frame as his lectures on natural theology at the Theological School, Vos affirmed the concept of *pure* and *mixed* articles. That is, pure articles are those truths that arise only from revelation whereas mixed articles flow both from reason and revelation. This is a distinction that substantively goes back to the theology of Aquinas.[150] With these principles in hand Vos argued, "We can certainly reason from the world up to God, but we cannot by logic descend from God to the world."[151] That Vos maintained the Princetonian apologetic methodology later in his career when

---

148. Abraham Kuyper, *Encyclopaedie Heilige Godgeleerdheid* (Amsterdam: J. A. Wormser, 1894), 3:456–64. Kuyper's view was not necessarily the default Dutch Reformed position, as others, such as J. J. Van Oosterzee (1817–1882), professor at the University of Utrecht, argued that apologetics took priority over theism in their respective order. See J. J. Van Oosterzee, *Christian Dogmatics: A Text-Book for Academical Instruction and Private Study*, trans. John Watson and Maurice J. Evans (New York: Scribner, Armstrong, 1874), 1:75–228; cf. Bavinck, "Recent Dogmatic Thought," 219–20.

149. There is evidence, however, that might suggest that Vos stands somewhere between Old Princeton and Kuyper on the place of apologetics. In his inaugural lecture at the Theological School, Vos states, "It [apologetics] is aimed not at those who stand outside, but at the brethren who have strayed, who have made themselves guilty of inconsistency, and unwittingly let in the enemy. Apologetics must not be abolished, it must for the time being be limited to our own sphere. It is our duty, wherever ideas are brought in that are undeniably in conflict with the starting point of our faith, to indefatigably bring this contradiction to light, so that those who have fallen in spite of themselves may see what kind of untenable position they hold." Vos, "Prospects of American Theology," 48. Whether Vos maintained this view throughout his career, or developed it, is unclear.

150. See J. V. Fesko, "The Scholastic Epistemology of Geerhardus Vos," *Reformed Faith & Practice* 3, no. 3 (2018): 21–45.

151. Vos, *Reformed Dogmatics*, 1:157.

he assumed the chair of biblical theology is evident in a 1906 essay he penned that argued for the need of both faith and biblical history:

> To join in the outcry against dogma and fact means to lower the ideal of what the Christian consciousness ought normally to be to the level of the spiritual depression of our own day and generation. How much better that we should all strive to raise our drooping faith and to reënrich our depleted experience up to the standard of those blessed periods in the life of the Church, when the belief in Bible history and the religion of the heart went hand in hand and kept equal pace, when people were ready to lay down their lives for facts and doctrines, because facts and doctrines formed the daily spiritual nourishment of their souls. May God by His Spirit maintain among us, and through our instrumentality revive around us, that truly evangelical type of piety which not merely tolerates facts and doctrines, but draws from them its strength and inspiration in life and service, its only comfort and hope in the hour of death.[152]

In other words, Vos, too, withstood both the Ritschlian tendency to sideline theoretical knowledge in favor of subjective religious knowledge and the mystical penchant to retreat to the testimony of the Spirit.[153] Faith and the facts of history were both necessary and thus played a role in apologetics, an enterprise informed by the insights of natural theology.

In short, Vos, the Princetonians, the Reformed orthodox, and the Reformers were plying the distinction between nature and grace, general and special revelation, creation and redemption. Or in biblical terms, Genesis begins with, "In the beginning *God*" (Gen. 1:1, emphasis added); in Pauline terms, Romans 1:19–20 comes before Romans 3:21. Thus Patton brooked no dissent from the so-called Christocentric theology of the late nineteenth century: "With those who in our day would make our theology more distinctively Christian by making it appear that our only knowledge of God comes to us through Christ, I have no sympathy."[154]

---

152. Geerhardus Vos, "Christian Faith and the Truthfulness of Bible History," *Princeton Theological Review* 4, no. 3 (1906): 304–5.

153. This is a theme in Patton's address on theological encyclopedia. See Patton, "Theological Encyclopaedia," 114–15.

154. Patton, "Theological Encyclopaedia," 115. Vos makes similar comments in his

While such a statement might at first strike the reader as impious, it instead rests on tried and true Reformed theological principles. Patton, the Princetonians, Vos, Kuyper, Bavinck, and the Reformed orthodox maintained the distinction between the *principium essendi* (foundation of being), namely, God, and the *principium cognoscendi theologiae* (foundation of knowing theology), namely, nature and Scripture.[155] God creates, and He reveals Himself both in creation and Scripture; to say, however, that we only know God through Christ conflates the *principia*—Christology swallows creation.

Vos's Historical Assessment of the Tradition

The second issue relates to Vos's assessment of the Reformed tradition's understanding of natural theology. In other words, how accurate is Vos's historiography? Vos's survey of the history of natural theology is relatively brief, and at times the answers to his questions only lightly touch upon figures and works. He notes that Augustine devoted extensive attention to natural theology and proved God's existence ontologically and through arguments that appealed to the innate knowledge of God (Q. 17). In his treatment of medieval theology, he makes a common nineteenth-century error by identifying scholasticism with specific theological positions, such as semi-Pelagianism (Q. 21), but he does not paint with such broad strokes so as to eliminate all nuance. He rightly recognizes that not all scholastics held the same views regarding faith and reason. Vos identifies Raymond of Sabunde as the father of

---

inaugural address. Vos, "Prospects of American Theology," 31. For likely Christocentric theologians that Patton and Vos have in mind, see Philip Schaff, *Theological Propaedeutic: A General Introduction to the Study of Theology* (New York: Scribner's, 1893), 362–63; Emanuel V. Gerhart, *Institutes of the Christian Religion*, (New York: Armstrong, 1891), 1:15–16, 48; Henry Boynton Smith, *System of Christian Theology* (New York: Scribner's, 1893), 91–105; cf. Richard A. Muller, "Henry Boynton Smith: Christocentric Theologian," *Journal of Presbyterian History* 61, no. 4 (1983): 429–44; Muller, "Emmanuel V. Gerhart on the 'Christ Idea' as Fundamental Principle," *Westminster Theological Journal* 48, no. 1 (1986): 97–117; Annette G. Aubert, *The German Roots of Nineteenth-Century American Theology* (Oxford: Oxford University Press, 2013), 71–72, 136–38. Also cf. Bavinck, "Theology of Albrecht Ritschl," 159; Ritschl, "Theology and Metaphysics," 187–88.

155. Muller, *Dictionary*, s.v. *principium essendi / principium cognoscendi* (p. 290).

natural theology (Q. 23.2) and notes that (1) he believed that natural theology must teach that God first exists and must therefore precede revealed theology, (2) that revealed theology teaches us what God says about Himself, and (3) that natural theology teaches us everything that is comprehended in the Bible but that we do not need first to believe everything on the basis of reason (Q. 24).

When Vos describes the sixteenth-century reception of natural theology, he makes the erroneous claim that the Reformation rejected it, though this description requires some untangling. Vos says,

> Was the Reformation favorable to the development of natural theology?
>
> No, for it opposed the Roman Catholic doctrine of tradition as well as the Semipelagianism of the Roman Catholic Church. For that reason, it preferred to stick to Scripture alone and wanted people not to rely on their own powers for their knowledge of God or to seek Him by their own means, but rather simply to believe in God. (Q. 25)

At one level, this description does not accord with the facts; the Reformation did not reject natural theology. At another level, Vos rightly notes that the Reformation rejected Roman Catholic views on tradition and its semi-Pelagian soteriology. A simple survey of key Reformation confessional documents can substantiate this claim. But to say that the Reformation stuck to Scripture alone does not accord with the evidence. Vos notes that both the Reformed and Lutheran churches only viewed natural theology as nothing more than an apologetic tool for use against unbelievers (Q. 28.1). Moreover, he observes that both Calvin and Philip Melanchthon (1497–1560) treated the subject, though Vos contends that Calvin placed less emphasis on the objective testimony of nature (QQ. 26–27). Such an admission reveals that the Reformation did not completely reject natural theology. Thus, Vos likely means to say that the Reformation rejected certain forms of Roman Catholic natural theology. That only certain forms were problematic appears to be Vos's point given the way that he describes Alsted's work and the internal and external books of nature, a view that echoes the earlier theme of Raymond of

Sabunde, which Vos says, "was increasingly lost from sight, to the detriment of natural theology" (Q. 29). The possibility exists, however, that there was an error on either the lecturer's or student's part in delivering or recording Vos's lecture at this point. So, while Vos's historiography contains some inaccuracies, on the whole he recognizes continuities and discontinuities between the patristic, medieval, Reformation, and post-Reformation periods. He does not completely dismiss natural theology out of hand.

Relationship to Later Reformed Thought

As the twentieth century dawned, Reformed opinions about the viability of natural theology began to shift. Karl Barth (1886–1968) was one of the first well-known theologians to voice dissent. In 1934 Barth famously debated Emil Brunner (1889–1966) in the midst of the rise of Nazism in Germany. Barth maintained that the church had to turn away from natural theology like one would avoid an abyss. For Barth the only source of theology was Christology; in his judgment natural theology would establish another focal point for theology other than Jesus Christ.[156] Despite his rejection of natural theology, Barth ironically was invited to give the 1937–1938 Gifford Lectures, a series devoted to the topic of natural theology. In his opening lecture Barth noted that speakers were supposed to address the topic "without reference to religion or upon any supposed special exception or so-called miraculous revelation."[157] Barth registered the idea that, as a Reformed theologian, he was subject to an ordinance that kept him away from natural theology, even if he was inclined toward the topic.[158] Nevertheless, Barth was not reticent and told the audience, "I am an avowed opponent of all natural theology."[159] Barth believed he

156. Andrew Moore, "Theological Critiques of Natural Theology," in *Oxford Handbook of Natural Theology*, 227–46 (here 234).

157. Karl Barth, *The Knowledge of God and the Service of God According to the Teaching of the Reformation: Recalling the Scottish Confession of 1560. The Gifford Lectures Delivered in the University of Aberdeen in 1937 and 1938*, trans. J. L. M. Haire and Ian Henderson (1938; repr., London: Hodder and Stoughton, 1960), 3.

158. Barth, *Knowledge of God*, 5.

159. Barth, *Knowledge of God*, 6.

was standing with the Reformation in his rejection, which contrasted with the compromises of modern Protestantism and Roman Catholicism with natural theology.[160] According to Barth, the Reformation stood in antithesis to natural theology, though he conceded that it made an occasional guarded and conditional use of the possibility of natural theology, as Calvin did in the opening chapters of his *Institutes*, or as Calvin and Martin Luther (1483–1546) did in their explanations of the law. Outliers notwithstanding, the Reformers sought to rest the church and salvation on the Word of God and on God's revelation in Jesus Christ alone.[161] Similar trends opposing natural theology unfolded in conservative Reformed circles.

When there was a realignment of the board of trustees at Princeton Seminary, J. Gresham Machen (1881–1937) led an exodus across the Delaware River to found Westminster Theological Seminary in Philadelphia, Pennsylvania. Machen was a product of Old Princeton and was out of step with the modernist shift within the institution. Machen explicitly stated that he agreed with the anthropology of Hodge and Warfield.[162] He believed that they promoted biblical truth but also admired and agreed with them on the role and place of apologetics in Reformed theology.[163] Machen also sat under the teaching of Francis Patton.[164] Like his Princeton professors, Machen objected to Ritschlian theology and the excising of metaphysics from theology for a "religion of humanity."[165] He was favorably disposed to the theistic proofs for the existence of God. In a similar fashion to Vos, Machen believed the proofs belonged to the discipline of philosophy, and therefore this

---

160. Barth, *Knowledge of God*, 8.

161. Barth, *Knowledge of God*, 8–9.

162. Paul Kjoss Helseth, "The Apologetical Tradition of the OPC: A Reconsideration," *Westminster Theological Journal* 60, no. 1 (1998): 109–29 (here 118).

163. J. Gresham Machen, "Christianity in Conflict," in *Contemporary American Theology*, ed. Virgilius Ferm (New York: Round Table, 1932), 1:245–74 (here 254).

164. W. Masselink, *Professor J. Gresham Machen: His Life and Defence of the Bible* [ThD diss., Free University of Amsterdam, 1938], 6.

165. Masselink, *Machen*, 26–27; cf. Ritschl, "Theology and Metaphysics," 154, 161–70, 177, 187–88.

discipline was of immense value to religion.[166] Machen sided with Patton and Warfield over and against Kuyper regarding the place and value of apologetics: "How, then, should the existence of such a God be established? The old answer to that question was that it should be established by the so-called 'theistic proofs,' in which an inference is drawn from the existence and from the character of the world to a personal Creator and Ruler. With these proofs must no doubt be included the 'moral argument' which infers from the presence of the moral law in the conscience of man the existence of a great Lawgiver."[167] When Machen writes of the "old answer," he is likely setting it up against several newer variants, such as Kuyper's and the Ritschlian understanding.

In fact, Machen specifically chides the Ritschlian notion that we "know God only through Christ," a point that places Machen in stark contrast to the later views of Barth.[168] Echoing Patton's earlier cited lecture on theological encyclopedia, Machen writes, "And so far as the intellectual defence of Christianity is concerned, the fact should never be obscured that theism is the logical prius of faith in Christ. 'Believe in God,' said Jesus, 'believe also in me.' To reverse that order, is to throw the entire organism of apologetics out of joint. The old order of apologetics is correct: first, there is a God; second, it is likely that He should reveal Himself; third, He has actually revealed Himself in Christ. It is a very serious fault when the last of these points is put first."[169] In line with early modern and the nineteenth-century views of Kuyper, Bavinck, and Vos, Machen believed that God revealed Himself in nature, human conscience, and Scripture.[170] Like Warfield, even though Machen believed that theism and natural theology logically preceded supernatural theology, he did not merely seek to establish a beachhead of bald theism. Rather, he wanted to press his case inland to assault the fortress of

---

166. J. Gresham Machen, "The Relation of Religion to Science and Philosophy," review of *Christianity at the Cross Roads*, by E. Y. Mullins, *Princeton Theological Review* 24, no. 1 (1926): 55; Masselink, *Machen*, 57.

167. Machen, "Relation," 55–56.

168. Machen, "Relation," 58.

169. Machen, "Relation," 59; Masselink, *Machen*, 57–58.

170. J. Gresham Machen, *What Is Faith?* (1925; repr., Edinburgh: Banner of Truth, 1996), 75–76; Masselink, *Machen*, 60.

unbelief. Machen writes, "We are pleading, in other words, for a truly comprehensive apologetic—an apologetic which does not neglect the theistic proofs or the historical evidence of the New Testament account of Jesus, but which also does not neglect the facts of the inner life of man. The force of such an apologetic is, we think, cumulative; such an apologetic is strong in its details; but it is even stronger because the details are embraced in a harmonious whole."[171] Machen believed that apologetics begins with theism but that "consistent Christianity is the easiest Christianity to defend, and that consistent Christianity—the only thoroughly Biblical Christianity—is found in the Reformed Faith." This was an idea that Machen learned from Warfield.[172] Machen expresses his agreement with the methods of Old Princeton, but at this point it appears that he does not delve beyond the nineteenth century to the early modern period to support his views. There is a sense in which Machen's natural theology and apologetics is a modern expression of early modern views with no effort to draw the two together. Despite Machen's agreement with his Old Princeton professors, one of the faculty members that Machen hired to teach apologetics at Westminster was of a different mind.

Machen hired Cornelius Van Til, who had an appreciation for the Old Princeton and early modern Reformed tradition. Van Til sought to take the basic common theme present in Kuyper, Bavinck, Warfield, and especially Machen, namely, employing the "full Christian faith and the self-attesting Scripture and build as best as we can upon it."[173] Despite the fact that some have tried to show how Van Til agreed with his Old Princeton and Dutch Reformed predecessors, in Van Til's mind, he had to raze much in the earlier tradition.[174] Van Til's criticisms are too numerous to expound in detail in this brief introduction, but a summary of them sufficiently demonstrates that he believed that he was headed in a new direction. Van Til maintained the following:

---

171. Machen, "Relation," 64–65; Masselink, *Machen*, 106.

172. Machen, "Christianity in Conflict," 254.

173. Cornelius Van Til, *A Christian Theory of Knowledge* (Phillipsburg, N.J.: Presbyterian and Reformed, 1969), 254.

174. VanDrunen, "Presbyterians, Philosophy, Natural Theology," 467.

1. Early modern Reformed scholasticism was an unholy wedding between orthodox theology and Aristotle—it was a form of rationalistic theology. Van Til wrote, "But after Calvin the everlasting temptation besetting all Christians, especially sophisticated Christians, to make friends with those that are of Cain's lineage proved too much for many Lutheran and even Reformed theologians and so Lutheran and Reformed Scholasticism were begotten and born." Hodge and Warfield were also guilty of scholasticism.[175] Such an unholy synthesis was akin to Israel's bond with the Philistines.[176]

2. Kuyper's and Bavinck's theologies were partially corrupted because "remnants of Scholasticism clung to their thinking." Bavinck's and Kuyper's views supposedly stood in contrast to Calvin's, which was set forth in the opening of his *Institutes*.[177] Both were untrue to their own Reformed theological presuppositions.[178] In Van Til's judgment, Kuyper and Bavinck were too similar to Aquinas.[179] In fact, they unwittingly endorsed "Rome's semi-Aristotelian epistemology influences."[180] Thus in Van Til's mind, he was being truly faithful to Bavinck and Kuyper when they were untrue to their own principles.[181]

3. His own apologetic method was a "genuine advance" over older scholastic methods through the idealist idea of "limiting concepts."[182] The Reformed church needed to "learn more and more to outgrow scholasticism in our notions about natural theology and natural ethics."[183]

4. Traditional apologetics "was based on some form of empiricist

---

175. Van Til, *Herman Dooyeweerd*, 3:17–18; Cornelius Van Til, *An Introduction to Systematic Theology* (Phillipsburg, N.J.: Presbyterian and Reformed, 1974), 30–42, 205.

176. Van Til, *Herman Dooyeweerd*, 3:23.

177. Cornelius Van Til, *The New Synthesis Theology of the Netherlands* (Phillipsburg, N.J.: Presbyterian and Reformed, 1975), 30, 36, 43.

178. Van Til, *Common Grace*, 36, 51–52.

179. Van Til, *Common Grace*, 44, 48–49; Van Til, *Defense of the Faith*, 294–95.

180. Van Til, *Common Grace*, 34.

181. Van Til, *Defense of the Faith*, 197, 208.

182. Van Til, *Common Grace*, 200.

183. Van Til, *Common Grace*, 94.

and/or rationalist philosophy. This was true, obviously, in the old Princeton apologetics. It was also true, to a lesser extent, in the Amsterdam apologetics as found in the writings of Kuyper, Bavinck, and Valentine Hepp (1879–1950). I tried to go 'beyond' these men, always with great appreciation for the work they had done, by *starting* from the authority of Christ speaking in Scripture as the presupposition of predication on any point, in any field of investigation."[184] Van Til even went as far as to agree with Barth regarding the true starting point of theology: "We must really do what Karl Barth has insisted that we must do but has not done, namely, start our interpretation of the whole of life *von oben* [from above]. We must begin our meditation upon any fact in the world in the light of the Son of God, the light which is as the light of the sun, the source of all other light."[185] Elsewhere Van Til states that a truly Protestant apologetic must begin with the presupposition of the triune God, as Calvin purportedly did in his *Institutes*. In this approach Calvin allegedly made a complete break with scholasticism.[186]

5. Warfield taught an apologetic methodology based on Butler's *Analogy*, in which there is an area of interpretation in which Christians and non-Christians can agree.[187] In Van Til's assessment, Butler was the same as Aquinas.[188]

6. Philosophical realism was problematic and hampered the theology and apologetics of Kuyper and Bavinck.[189] Instead, Van

184. Cornelius Van Til, "Response to G. C. Berkouwer," in *Jerusalem and Athens: Critical Discussions on the Theology and Apologetics of Cornelius Van Til*, ed. E. R. Geehan (Phillipsburg, N.J.: Presbyterian and Reformed, 1980), 203–4. See also Van Til, "Response to Herman Dooyeweerd," in *Jerusalem and Athens*, 98; Van Til, *Defense of the Faith*, 197.

185. Cornelius Van Til, *The Reformed Pastor and Modern Thought* (Phillipsburg, N.J.: Presbyterian and Reformed, 1980), 196.

186. Van Til, *Defense of the Faith*, 179; Cornelius Van Til, *Christianity in Conflict* (1962; repr., Glenside, Pa.: Westminster Campus Bookstore, 1996), 3:26–27, 30.

187. Van Til, *Common Grace*, 183.

188. Van Til, *Defense of the Faith*, 4, 194, 218.

189. Cornelius Van Til, "Response to Richard Gaffin," in *Jerusalem and Athens*, 239;

Til believed that Kantian idealism represented a watershed for apologetics: "This is the significance of Kant's 'Copernican Revolution.' It is only in our day that there can therefore be anything like a fully consistent presentation of one system of interpretation over against the other. For the first time in history the stage is set for a head-on collision. There is now a clear-cut antithesis between the two positions."[190]

7. Traditional apologetics offered no possibility of truly confronting unbelief.[191]
8. Because of its alignment with Rome, Aristotle, and pagan elements of thought, the apologetics of Old Princeton could only arrive at a general form of theism, not Christian theism.[192]
9. He was in favor of the views of Kuyper over and against Warfield on the place of apologetics.[193]
10. Old Princeton and Amsterdam rightly echoed Calvin's concept of the *sensus divinitatis*.[194]
11. The Trinity is the *principium essendi* of knowledge.[195]
12. Bavinck's and Kuyper's use of common notions was erroneous.[196]

Despite all of these pointed disagreements with Old Princeton and Amsterdam, some have claimed that Van Til's apologetic stands in continuity with them on natural theology and apologetics.[197]

Van Til, *Common Grace*, 45; Van Til, *Introduction to Systematic Theology*, 44–46.

190. Cornelius Van Til, introduction to *The Inspiration and Authority of the Bible*, by Benjamin B. Warfield, ed. Samuel G. Craig (repr., Phillipsburg, N.J.: Presbyterian and Reformed, 1948), 23–24.

191. Van Til, *Defense of the Faith*, 207, 285; Van Til, *Introduction to Systematic Theology*, 117.

192. Van Til, *Defense of the Faith*, 220.

193. Van Til, *Defense of the Faith*, 265; Van Til, introduction to *Inspiration and Authority*, 2–3.

194. Van Til, *Defense of the Faith*, 297.

195. Van Til, introduction to *Inspiration and Authority*, 10.

196. Van Til, *Introduction to Systematic Theology*, 47.

197. See, e.g., Donald MacLeod, "Bavinck's *Prolegomena*: Fresh Light on Amsterdam, Old Princeton, and Cornelius Van Til," *Westminster Theological Journal* 68 (2006):

Regardless of what agreement might exist between Van Til, Old Princeton, and Amsterdam, there are three irrefutable evidences of disagreement. First, Van Til emphatically disagreed with them. He rejected scholasticism; he repudiated Reformed orthodox views on natural theology because of their supposedly profane alliance with Aquinas and Rome; he rebuked Bavinck and Kuyper for the same reasons; he moved beyond Old Princeton because of its allegedly rationalist apologetic. Van Til believed he was moving beyond the tradition and outgrowing its compromised theology. In Van Til's evaluation, he was the only truly consistent Calvinist. Second, the flowering of historical theological scholarship on the relationship between the Middle Ages, the Reformation, and Reformed orthodoxy reveals Van Til's erroneous historiography. The fact that he identified scholasticism with rationalism instead of seeing it as a method of doing theology illustrates the problematic character of his historiography. Van Til saw no difference between Aquinas and Butler, for example; he failed to factor the significant philosophical and theological differences between the thirteenth and nineteenth centuries. Moreover, to say that Calvin begins with the doctrine of God fails to account for the Genevan's appeal to the pagan arguments of Cicero in the opening books of his *Institutes*. Third, even though there are common elements in the apologetics and natural theology of Van Til, Old Princeton, and Amsterdam, the fact remains that Van Til's starting point is formally different than that of his predecessors. In agreement with Barth, Van Til began from above with the self-attesting Christ of Scripture, whereas Old Princeton and Amsterdam began with theism. This is a formal difference between them, as Warfield, Patton, Machen, and Bavinck, for example, did not scuttle their Trinitarian Reformed theology in their apologetics or natural theology. Rather, from a foundation of Scripture they put natural revelation to use as their lead argument. In

261–82 (here 263–64, 271, 272); Helseth, "Apologetical Tradition," 109–10, 125–27; Nathaniel Gray Sutanto, "From Antithesis to Synthesis: A Neo-Calvinistic Theological Strategy in Herman Bavinck and Cornelius Van Til," *Journal of Reformed Theology* 9, no. 4 (2015): 348–74 (esp. 368–71); Sutanto, "Neo-Calvinism on General Revelation: A Dogmatic Sketch," *International Journal of Systematic Theology* 20, no. 4 (2018): 495–516; cf. Muller, "Kuyper and Bavinck," 6.

this vein they look very much like Van Til, but Van Til did not believe this was a merely formal but substantive difference and consequently fatal flaw.

Thus, even though some might advance the claim that Vos was the Van Tillian morning star, there is no question that Vos's lectures on natural theology fall in line with the views of Old Princeton and Amsterdam, not those of Van Til.[198] Vos's lectures arguably contain nothing adumbrating Van Til's distinctive position, but instead reflect the natural theology of the Reformation, Reformed orthodox, Old Princeton, and Amsterdam. Moreover, nothing in the Vos corpus hints that Vos's views on natural theology or the place of apologetics changed later in his career.

Prospects of a Future Reformed Natural Theology

The recovery of Vos's lectures on natural theology inherently raises the question of whether the Reformed natural-theology project ought to be reopened.[199] Despite the noisy din of their objections, the Barthian and Van Tillian dismissals of Reformed natural theology should be set aside. Their objections should not, however, be set aside because of a devotion to tradition. Tradition in its worst sense is when the living profess the dead faith of their ancestors and substitute the doctrines of men for the teaching of God—the dead faith of the living. The best form of tradition is the living faith of the dead, where the church harvests the wisdom, insights, and exegesis of earlier generations. If the church fathers, medieval theologians, Reformers, Reformed orthodox, and nineteenth-century Reformed theologians all promoted a biblically subordinated *theologia naturalis regenitorum*, then the twentieth-century rejection of such stands as the outlier, not the biblical norm. With Vos we must recognize that natural theology "does, however, directly teach many things that Scripture does not so much explicitly teach as assume" (Q. 12.2), and it "teaches us to adore the wisdom of God in nature, His ways and

198. See, e.g., William Dennison, *In Defense of the Eschaton: Essays in Reformed Apologetics*, ed. James Douglas Baird (Eugene, Ore.: Wipf & Stock, 2015), xi–xii, 30, 31, 33, 34, 35, 48, 49, 94, 98n33, 130, 137, 158, 161.

199. See also VanDrunen, "Presbyterians, Philosophy, Natural Theology," 468–69.

His works (Q. 12.3). Therefore, we must consult God's book of nature. The supposedly devastating Humean and Kantian blows against the proofs for the existence of God were against rationalist versions, not those of Augustine, Aquinas, and the early modern Reformed tradition. Rent from special revelation, the proofs were vulnerable to attack and thus crumbled because the pillar of special revelation had been removed. Despite the criticisms against the proofs, such as the complaint that they only lead to bald theism, the historic Reformed tradition has maintained that one can begin with theism, but such arguments are incomplete unless they terminate in the full-fledged Christian theism, a theism that terminates in Christ. In conjunction with supernatural theology, therefore, natural theology can refute "those who have rejected the supernatural revelation of God" (Q. 12.4). While recovering natural theology will undoubtedly take at least a generation, the Reformed church should return *ad fontes,* mine the treasures of the past, publish works on natural theology, and reintegrate it in the theological curriculum. Such an enterprise is not merely to repristinate the tradition but to ply the best minds of the church to study God's book of nature and read it in concert with the book of Scripture.

OUTLINE

76–77. The theory of development
78–80. Theory of revelation
81–84. Theory of inference
85–91. Theory of intuition

III. A Discussion of the Ontological Argument (QQ. 92–114)
92–94. Definition
95–105. Anselm
106–109. Descartes and Spinoza
110–114. Kant and later

IV. A Discussion of the Cosmological Argument (QQ. 115–131)
115–118. Definition and introduction
119–122. Objections: Kant, Hume, and Mill
123–131. The argument formulated and critiqued

V. A Discussion of the Physico-Teleological Argument (QQ. 132–150)
132–139. Definition and argument
140–150. Objections and responses

VI. A Discussion of the Ethical Argument (QQ. 151–174)
151–158. Conscience and the ethical argument
159–161. Rejection of Schopenhauer, Hobbes, and Bain on the origins of conscience
162–172. Utilitarian or hedonistic theory
173–174. Evolutionary ethicists

VII. A Discussion of the Religious Argument (QQ. 175–204)
175–176. The old argument from the agreement of nations
177–188. Religion as a psychological phenomenon: emotion, "feeling"; objections
189–190. Religion as derived from fear
191–193. Religion in relation to will and morality
194–195. Feuerbach
196–204. Religion defined in relation to the arguments for the existence of God

The Immortality of the Soul (QQ. 205–224)

205–217. The essence of the soul: various theories

218–221. The metaphysical argument for the immortality of the soul

222. The ethical argument

223. The religious argument

224. The historical argument

LECTURE NOTES ON NATURAL THEOLOGY

Prolegomenon

The Systems of Religion

The Immortality of the Soul

PROLEGOMENON

Natural Theology[1]

1. Where does natural theology correspond with revealed theology, and where is it distinguished from the latter?
It corresponds with revealed theology in that both have the same object—that is, God. It is distinguished from revealed theology in that its source of knowledge and method of treatment differ—that is, they are taken from nature, as indicated by the adjective "natural."

2. How then do you define "natural theology"?
As a theology—that is, a teaching concerning God—that takes its content and method from nature.

3. What do you understand by "nature"?
All that is subject to the normal link between causes and effects, and that works according to fixed laws, from the beginning of creation.

4. What then are the marks[2] of the concept of "nature"?
Regularity and continuity (i.e., constancy and uninterruptedness).

---

1. DG inserts here:

"Contents of Natural Theology:
I. God's existence and unity
II. God's nature or attributes
III. God's acts
IV. The immortality of the soul."

This is omitted in V and A. The list in DG is not representative of the organization of Vos's lectures; rather, they indicate the topics traditionally found in Reformed natural theologies. Vos's lectures do not include sections on the unity, nature, attributes, or acts of God. See QQ. 92–204 on the existence of God and religion; see QQ. 205–224 on the immortality of the soul.

2. V and A: "marks" (*kenmerken*); DG erroneously reads: "concepts" (*begrippen*).

5. *How can you confirm this from the etymology of the word "nature"?*
Natura comes from *nascor*, "to be born." What is born is subject to this law of regularity and uninterruptedness.

6. *Do human acts of free will likewise belong to ⌜the sphere of⌝[3] nature?*
Certainly, for regardless of what the cause of acts of free will may be, they are not unrelated to the character of the human race, and the human race is only one link in the chain of nature, and its life is bound by fixed laws.

7. *If you were to integrate this concept of nature into the above definition, what would the result be?*
"Natural theology" is a knowledge of God that takes its content and method from the world as it presents itself to us as governed by fixed laws.

8. *What is in more or less precise terms[4] the difference between natural and revealed theology?*
⌜According to the above, there is a twofold distinction⌝:[5]

1. Revealed theology comes to us on the basis of something that is new and unusual. Revelation is always something that enters the world[6] anew and apart from the regular causality of nature. For this reason, revelation is accompanied by miracles to make it knowable. The consequences—i.e., the content of revelation—may remain; revelation itself—i.e., the act of revelation—is of a passing nature.
2. Revelation is something that does not remain continually, while nature continually bears witness. Psalm 19:1–4: "Day to day pours out speech abundantly, and night to night reveals knowledge."

3. So V and A; omitted in DG.

4. V and A: "more or less precisely" (*eenigszins nauwkeurig*); DG: "precisely" (*eens nauwkeurig*).

5. So DG; omitted in V and A.

6. DG and V: "the world" (*de wereld*); A: "nature" (*de natuur*).

9. How then do you understand "revelation" in contrast with "nature"?
Not in the wide[7] sense of everything that God has revealed to us about Himself, ⌜since this would include nature itself,⌝[8] but rather in the narrower sense as God's special intervention whereby He in a direct way and through special means gives people a knowledge of Himself that they cannot obtain from nature as their only source.

10. Does Scripture teach that there is a natural knowledge of God?
Yes, in passages like Psalm 19:1–4; 94:8–10; Acts 14:15–17; 17:24–29; Romans 1:19–21. These passages also teach that this natural revelation is sufficiently clear to hold people accountable before God concerning their religion, "so that they are without excuse."[9]

11. What does Scripture teach about the sufficiency or insufficiency of this revelation in nature unto salvation?
It teaches that natural knowledge is insufficient: 1 Corinthians 1:21; Galatians 2:21; 3:21; Acts 4:12; John 3:36; Romans 11:13–15.

12. What value does natural theology still have then?

1. Negatively, it cannot teach believers anything unto salvation that is not contained in Scripture.
2. It does, however, directly teach many things that Scripture does not so much explicitly teach as assume.
3. It teaches us to adore the wisdom of God in nature, His ways[10] and His works. Psalm 104.
4. Natural theology owes its position in science to its use in apologetics, for refuting those who have rejected the supernatural revelation of God.

---

7. DG and A: "wide" (*wijden*); V: "widest" (*wijdste*).
8. So V and A; omitted in DG.
9. Rom. 1:20.
10. DG and A: "ways" (*wegen*); V: "essence" (*wezen*).

13. What is the relationship between natural theology and metaphysics?
Natural theology can be viewed also as a part of philosophy, and as such represents the transition between philosophy and theology. Metaphysics is likewise a part of philosophy. However, metaphysics treats the first principles *of being as such,* while natural theology treats them as they find their unity in God's thoughts and acts.

14. What has the relationship between systematic theology (dogmatics) and natural theology historically been like?
For a long time no distinction was made between these two sciences, since all systematic theology had become a kind of philosophy, that is, a natural science. Many of the church fathers sought to elevate faith to knowledge, to turn *pistis* into *gnosis.* The same holds true for the scholastics of the Middle Ages. The church fathers were always motivated in this by apologetic reasons. They were looking for a theology that they could use to convince their pagan opponents.

15. List several arguments of natural theology that the church fathers already used.

1. *The argument from analogy:* just like animals and people are ruled by a single individual, so it is also likely that there is a single ruler of the world. This is an argument that was directed against polytheism.

2. *Ontological arguments:* these attempt to derive the existence of God from the concept of God as an infinite, ⸢eternal,⸣[11] omnipotent being.

3. *Historical arguments:* these move from the orderly course of world history to the existence of God as governor.

4. *Cosmological arguments:* these ascend from the changes in the world to a first cause.

---

11. So V and A; omitted in DG.

16. What difference was there in the inclination of the Greek and Latin churches when it came to the relationship between natural and revealed theology?

The Greek church constantly sought to unite philosophy and gospel. The Latin church, and Tertullian in particular, sought to contrast the two most sharply as if they were irreconcilable.[12] This is related to each church's respective character. The Greek church was speculative, and Platonic philosophy reigned uncontested in it. This is why the Greek church addressed issues pertaining to theology proper, such as the essence of God, the Trinity, and Christology. The Latin church, however, bore the mark of Roman jurisprudence, was practical in its orientation, and therefore attempted to develop the issues relating to the justice of God, to sin, and to salvation (Augustine, Pelagius). Since for the latter issues it is the Bible alone that gives insight, while for the former group also philosophy offers some degree of insight as well, ⸢the Greek church preferred to view theology and philosophy as one, while⸣[13] the Latin church saw them as distinct.

17. Was there no exception to this general rule in the Western church?

Yes, Augustine devoted extensive attention to natural theology.[14] He began by proving the existence of God ontologically. It likewise bears observing here that there was general acceptance of innate knowledge of God also in the West.

18. What was specific to the theology of Dionysius the Areopagite, the sixth-century mystic?[15]

He taught in a pantheistic sense that one actually cannot know anything about God, who is exalted above all negation and affirmation, but that

12. Tertullian, *Prescription against Heretics*, in *The Ante-Nicene Fathers*, ed. Alexander Roberts and James Donaldson (repr., Grand Rapids: Eerdmans, 1950), 3:383–431.

13. So DG and V; erroneously omitted in A.

14. See, e.g., Augustine, *The City of God*, trans. Marcus Dods (1950; repr., New York: Modern Library, 1978), bk. 6 (pp. 182ff.).

15. See Pseudo-Dionysius, *The Complete Works*, trans. Colm Luibhéid (Mahwah, N.J.: Paulist Press, 1988).

negations still come closer to the truth than affirmations do. It is easier to define God as He is not, than as He is.

19. Who later continued this negative line of argumentation?
John of Damascus, the last great theologian of the Eastern church (700–750). He assembled[16] all negative elements into a single great argument so as to conclude that God exists as creator, sustainer, ruler, and artist of the universe, incorporeal, without origin, immutable, incorruptible.[17]

20. How did the attempts undertaken by the fathers to rationalize theology differ from those of the medieval scholastics?
The fathers were motivated by a practical intention, for the scholastics there was a scientific reason. The former wanted to refute their opponents, the latter to understand.

21. Was the pursuit of the scholastics also related to their semi-Pelagianism?
Yes, whenever the human race ⸢and human reason⸣[18] are not viewed as entirely corrupt, it becomes easier to try to build a theology on the basis of human reason alone. When Augustine's doctrine of human corruption was revived during the Reformation, people once again became suspicious of reason and sought recourse in Scripture as the source of theology.

22. Did all scholastics hold the same view on reason as a source of knowledge for theology?
No.

1. Some taught that faith does not depend on reason. They already believed apart from all rational proof, but still sought rational satisfaction so as also to demonstrate *a posteriori* by reason what had already been established apart from reason.

---

16. V and A: "assembled" (*verzamelde*); DG: "changed" (*veranderde*).

17. John of Damascus, *On the Orthodox Faith*, 1.3, in *A Select Library of Nicene and Post-Nicene Fathers of the Christian Church*, ed. Philip Schaff and Henry Wace, 2nd series (repr., Grand Rapids: Eerdmans, 1952), vol. 9, pt. 2, pp. 2–3.

18. So V and A; omitted in DG.

Such demonstration was no practical necessity for them, but a theoretical pleasure (Anselm).

2. Others, like Abelard, were of the view that the truths of faith do not gain practical certainty for us until they are demonstrated on rational grounds. They were thus rationalists in the negative sense of the word.

23. *Which of the later scholastics do we explicitly need to mention here?*

1. Durandus of Saint-Pourçain (d. 1333): He seems to have been the first to distinguish explicitly between the three well-known ways for arriving at a natural theology:[19] a. the way of eminence; b. the way of causality;[20] and c. the way of negation.
2. Raymond of Sabunde owes his importance to his work entitled *The Book of Nature or of Creatures*.[21] He lived in the middle of the fifteenth century. He is particularly important for the clear distinction he drew between the book of nature and the book of Scripture. Raymond thus considered nature a book, that is, something designed to speak the truth. This view has in a certain sense earned him the right to be called the father of natural theology.

24. *How did Raymond view the relationship between natural and revealed theology?*

1. Natural theology must ⸢first⸣[22] teach us that there is a God who exists, and in terms of necessity therefore precedes revealed theology.
2. Revealed theology can then teach us what God says about Himself.

---

19. DG: "natural theology" (*Theologia Naturalis*); V and A: "natural knowledge of God" (*Natuurlijke Godskennis*).

20. DG and A: "causality" (*oorzakelijkheid*); V: "necessity" (*noodzakelijkheid*).

21. Raymond of Sabunde, *Theologia Naturalis, sive Liber Creaturarum* (n.p.: Martinus Flach, 1496).

22. So V and A; omitted in DG.

3. In terms of extent as well, natural theology teaches us everything that is comprehended in the Bible, although we do not first need to believe everything on the basis of reason.

25. Was the Reformation favorable to the development of natural theology?
No, for it opposed the Roman Catholic doctrine of tradition as well as the semi-Pelagianism of the Roman Catholic Church. For that reason, it preferred to stick to Scripture alone and wanted people not to rely on their own powers for their knowledge of God or to seek Him by their own means, but rather simply to believe in God.

26. What is the unusual position that Calvin holds in this matter?
Although he accepts an irradicable, innate desire for God in humankind, he still places less emphasis on the objective testimony that nature bears toward God, and he seems to think that it is only when nature is connected to our innate idea of God that it gives us an intelligible testimony—which even then is more serviceable to the practical adoration of God's wisdom than it is to theoretical ends.[23]

27. What was Melanchthon's position on natural theology?
In the first edition of his theology, he did not use any of the arguments derived from reason or nature.[24] Later on he offered a somewhat confused list of relevant issues in his doctrine of creation. By the 1543 edition, however, his treatment [of natural theology] had become careful and ordered, although it remained incomplete and still appeared to be of secondary importance.

28. How did natural theology develop after the Reformation?

1. Neither the Reformed churches nor the Lutheran churches viewed natural theology as anything more than an apologetic

23. Cf. John Calvin, *Institutes of the Christian Religion*, trans. Henry Beveridge (Edinburgh: Calvin Translation Society, 1845), 1.3.1.

24. Cf. Philip Melanchthon, *Common Places: Loci Communes 1521*, trans. Christian Preus (St. Louis, Mo.: Concordia, 2014); Melanchthon, *Loci Theologici Recens Recogniti* (Wittenberg: Petrus Seitz, 1543), fols. E1ff.

means against unbelievers. They also did not grant that natural theology represents an introduction to revealed theology for Christians.

2. Among the Lutherans ⸢in particular,⸣[25] theology was considered to be the doctrine of salvation, that is, soteriology. Nature teaches nothing about salvation. Therefore, it can produce no true theology.
3. In their Christology and teaching on the Lord's Supper, the Lutherans also had other reasons to ⸢despise and⸣[26] disregard the testimony of reason and the natural senses. This explains why there is greater aversion to natural theology among them than there is among the Reformed.

29. Who first brought improvement to this situation?
Alsted, who in 1615 published his *Natural Theology*. He speaks of an internal book of nature (the conscience, etc.) and an external book of nature (the ⸢objective⸣[27] testimony of creation).[28] Later on the latter was increasingly lost from sight, to the detriment of natural theology.

30. How can the predilection for and treatment of this innate idea of God be explained?
By the influence of Cartesian philosophy, in which the idea of God plays an important role. Descartes (1596–1650) needed the idea of God to guarantee certainty for the reliability of the rest of our[29] knowledge.[30] It is only if God exists that I can be certain that my reason and my senses are not deceiving me. He therefore did not use this idea of God for religious

25. So V and A; omitted in DG.
26. So V and A; omitted in DG.
27. So V and A; omitted in DG.
28. Johannes Heinrich Alsted, *Theologica Naturalis* (Frankfurt: Antonius Hummius, 1615).
29. V and A: "our" (*onzer*); DG: "his" (*zijner*).
30. René Descartes, *Meditations on First Philosophy*, trans. Donald A. Cress, 3rd ed. (Indianapolis: Hackett, 1993), Meditation 3 (pp. 24–34), Meditation 5 (pp. 42–46).

or theological reasons, but for purely philosophical considerations. As a result, natural theology became the maidservant of philosophy.

31. Was this servitude altogether fruitless?
No, a host of treatises on natural theology appeared in both the Reformed and Lutheran churches.

32. Was the relationship between natural and revealed theology always accurately described?
No, some claimed that reason and the natural theology derived from it had to serve to demonstrate the divine origin ⌜of the Scriptures and⌝[31] of divine revelation in the narrower sense, and that our faith in both in the end depends on reason.

33. What influence did Leibnizian-Wolffian philosophy have on natural theology?
People took their rationalizing even further and attempted to derive all theology from formal, abstract principles, especially in an ontological sense. At first they restricted themselves to the innate idea, but later proceeded entirely from logical concepts. This development was joined by the strictly geometrical method. Science was no longer governed by the object, but by the method. This explains Wolff's demand that every treatment of natural theology restrict itself to a single argument.

34. Who brought an end to all these rationalistic speculations?
Immanuel Kant (1724–1804). Initially a rationalist from the Leibnizian-Wolffian school, he remained one in the deeper sense of the term. His most important works are: 1. *Critique of Pure Reason*, 1781; 2. *Critique of Practical Reason*, 1782; 3. *Prolegomena*, 1783; 4. *Critique of Judgment*, 1790.[32]

---

31. So DG and V; omitted in A.

32. Immanuel Kant, *Critique of Pure Reason*, trans. Paul Guyer and Allen W. Wood (Cambridge: Cambridge University Press, 1998); Kant, *Critique of Practical Reason*, trans. Mary Gregor (Cambridge: Cambridge University Press, 1997); Kant, *The Prolegomena to Any Future Metaphysics*, trans. Gary Hatfield, rev. ed. (Cambridge: Cambridge University

35. *Give a brief overview of Kant's system.*[33]

1. In their knowledge, human beings are receptive and spontaneous, at once passive and active. They are receptive in terms of the content which they receive through sensible impressions. They are spontaneous ⸢or active⸣[34] in terms of the form in which they grasp and process these impressions. The forms are twofold, namely forms of intuition and forms of understanding.

2. Since the forms are not in the things outside of us, but are applied by us to the impressions which we receive from things, those things do not appear to us as they are in themselves but as we make them by distortion. What we know are only phenomena, not the things as they exist in themselves. Our knowledge is phenomenalistic.

3. However, since these forms do not differ between [person] A and [person] B, they do achieve a certain agreement in the knowledge of all people. Science must always be something certain and common. Until that time, the scientific character of our knowledge had always been located in its agreement with reality. Kant now located it in the agreement which our knowledge has with the forms of intuition and understanding. This is called the immanent concept of truth.

4. The forms of intuition and understanding relate to experience alone and are intended only for it. Yet human beings have within their mind a natural and ⸢inevitable⸣[35] inclination to apply these forms to something that lies beyond our experience, that is, to the totality of things. This ability is what Kant calls "reason," in distinction from "understanding." He therefore has intuition, understanding, and reason. Reason forms the ideas, which are three in number: the idea of the soul as

---

Press, 2004); Kant, *Critique of the Power of Judgment,* ed. Paul Guyer, trans. Paul Guyer and Eric Matthews (Cambridge: Cambridge University Press, 2006).

33. Cf. James McCosh, *The Prevailing Types of Philosophy: Can They Logically Reach Reality* (New York: Scribner, 1890), 18–36.

34. So V and A; omitted in DG.

35. So V and A; omitted in DG.

a permanent substance; the idea of the world as an endless chain of causes and effects; and the idea of God as the most perfect Being. Since the content of these ideas lies beyond all experience, they have no theoretical validity. The idea of the soul is based on a psychological paralogism, since the unity of the self-conscious *I* is exchanged for the unity and absolute permanence of a soul substance. The idea of the world leads to mutually destructive antinomies. The idea of God, as it is demonstrated in rational theology,[36] rests entirely on sophisms. The ideas do have practical value, however, inasmuch as they contain a collateral testimony for what practical reason teaches.

5. The fundamental law of practical reason is that the good must exist and that there must be correspondence between the good and happiness, that is, the good must be happy. According to Kant, this law presumes three things: (a) I must, so I also can = freedom of the will. (b) In my pursuit I only attain the morally good infinitely slowly; if I am to attain the morally good, my life cannot be finite = I am immortal. (c) Even though I am moral, I cannot guarantee my happiness, meaning that there must be a higher being that accomplishes it = God exists. As such, Kant reconstructs using practical reason what he had torn down in the *Critique of Pure Reason*. These three—i.e., God, freedom, and immortality—are called the postulates of practical reason.

6. According to Kant, religion is in its entirety an element and tool of morality. Religion is the fulfillment of our duties as God's commands.[37] Kant understood doctrines allegorically, thereby turning them into means of morality.

---

36. V and A: "rational theology" (*rationale theologie*); DG: "natural theology" (*Theologia Naturalis*).

37. The sentence is not identified as a quotation by V, DG, or A, but part of the sentence appears in Q. 191 (V and DG) with quotation marks around the predicate. Cf. Kant, *Critique of Practical Reason*, 107–8: "In this way the moral law leads through the concept of the highest good, as the object and final end of pure practical reason, *to religion, that is, to the recognition* [Ger., *Erkenntnis*; Vos translates as "fulfillment"] *of all duties as divine commands*" (italics in the original).

36. What was the outcome of Kant's critique?

The common proofs for the existence of God were severely discredited. So, too, the pantheistic development of German philosophy after Kant robbed theology of its right of independent existence.

37. What was the main form in which natural theology was treated in England?

The English largely devoted themselves to physico-theology, which is the investigation of the order in nature so as to arrive at the existence of a creator of order. The year 1802 saw the appearance of William Paley's famous *Natural Theology*.[38] This trajectory was likewise favored in the Bridgewater treatises.[39] See also Thompson's *Principles of Natural Theology* (1857) and his *Christian Theism*.[40]

38. What is the title of the important work that has recently appeared in Germany?

Ulrici's *Gott und die Natur*.[41]

39. What unusual method does O. Zöckler follow in his Theologia Naturalis, published in 1860?[42]

He attempted to demonstrate that nature is governed by the same laws which Scripture holds forth to us in the spiritual realm. On the basis of this agreement, he then attempted to prove the existence of God

---

38. William Paley, *Natural Theology or Evidence and the Existence and Attributes of the Deity, Collected from the Appearances of Nature*, ed. Matthew D. Eddy and David Knight (Oxford: Oxford University Press, 2006).

39. A series of eight treatises "On the Power, Wisdom, and Goodness of God, as manifested in the Creation" funded in the last will and testament of Francis Henry, Earl of Bridgewater, on which see J. Topham, "Beyond the 'Common Context': The Production and Reading of the Bridgewater Treatises," *Isis* 89, no. 2 (1998): 233–62.

40. Robert Anchor Thompson, *Principles of Natural Theology* (London: Rivingtons, 1857); Thompson, *Christian Theism: The Testimony of Reason and Revelation to the Existence and Character of the Supreme Being*, 2 vols. (London: Rivingtons, 1855).

41. Hermann Ulrici, *Gott und die Natur* (Leipzig: I. D. Weigel, 1862).

42. Otto Zöckler, *Theologia Naturalis: Entwurf einer Systematischen Naturtheologie* (Frankfurt: Herder & Zimmer, 1860).

teleologically as the one who effected this agreement, as well as the reliability of the revelation in Scripture.

40. What factor has recently returned to the foreground in the treatment of natural theology?

The philosophy of history, meaning that people are attempting to demonstrate that an orderly development can be discerned in history, that it witnesses guidance and a purpose. Since human beings themselves have reached no such agreement for order but each person works without a prior agreement with the others, we must assume that this plan is being executed by a higher, all-governing mind—that is, that God governs history. This is thus a specific application of the teleological argument to the social and historical life of the human race.

41. Is this an old view?

Traces of the argument from history can be found in Irenaeus, Tertullian, Clement of Alexandria, Augustine, and others. However, as a distinct discipline, the philosophy of history is a product of modernity, since people in former times were not in a state where they could obtain a sufficiently wide overview of world history and were forced to restrict themselves to specific groups by the gaps in their knowledge of language and geography. A more comprehensive view first began to emerge with Herder (*Ideën zur Philosophie und zur Geschichte der Menschkeit*, 1784), Hegel (*Vorlesungen über die Philosophie der Geschichte*), Bunsen (*Gott in der Geschichte*, 1852–1858), and Guizot.[43]

---

43. Johann Gottfried von Herder, *Ideën zur Philosophie und Geschichte der Menschkeit* (Leipzig: J. F. Hartknoch, 1841); G. W. F. Hegel, *Vorlesungen über die Philosophie der Geschichte* (Leipzig: Philipp Reclam, 1982); Hegel, *Lectures on the Philosophy of World History*, trans. H. B. Nisbet (Cambridge: Cambridge University Press, 1984); Christian Karl Josias Bunsen, *Gott in der Geschichte* (Leipzig: F. U. Brodhaus, 1858); Bunson, *God in History; Or, the Progress of Man's Faith in the Moral Order of the World*, 3 vols. (London: Longmans, Green, 1868–1870); François Guizot, *Meditations sur l'essence de la religion chretienne* (Paris: Michel Lévy, 1864); Guizot, *Méditations sur l'état actuel de la religion chrétienne* (Paris: Michel Lévy, 1866); also Guizot, *Meditations on the Essence of Christianity, and on the Religious Questions of the Day* (London: John Murray, 1864).

42. To what extent can we say that theology's modern transformation into a science of religion has had a negative impact on natural theology?

The so-called science of religion does not concern itself with what corresponds to the object of religion (i.e., God), but with religion as a subjective phenomenon in the human race for which it seeks a natural explanation. Even apart from the fact that the science of religion is therefore no theology but rather belongs to psychology, of everything that constitutes the content or subject of natural theology, it can treat only the part that is in human nature.[44]

---

44. V: "that is in human nature" (*dat in d. mensch. natuur is*); DG and A are both incomplete here: "that in the human" (DG includes ellipses to reflect the error here: *dat in de menschelijke… … …*; A ends abruptly and illogically: *dat in de menschel.*).

THE SYSTEMS OF RELIGION

43. In what order are the various issues that present themselves to us here best treated?

We will offer:

I. A historical overview of the different systems of religion and religious faith (question 44).
II. A critical overview of the theories that seek to explain the rise and development of religion (question 75).
III. A discussion of the ontological argument (question 92).
IV. A discussion of the cosmological argument (question 115).
V. A discussion of the physico-teleological[1] argument (question 132).
VI. A discussion of the ethical argument (question 151).
VII. A discussion of the religious argument (question 175).

I. A Historical Overview of the Different Systems of Religion and Religious Faith

44. How are the various systems of religion and religious faith best divided?

A first distinction can be made between monism, pluralism, and atheism. Monism can in turn be divided into pantheism, deism, monotheism, and theism. Pluralism can be divided into dualism and polytheism, while atheism can assume widely differing forms but is not, strictly speaking, a scientific theory.

---

1. A: "physico-teleological" (*physico-teleologisch*); DG and V: "physico-theological" (*Physico-theologisch*).

Monism

45. What does the term "monism"[2] mean?

It is derived from the Greek word *monos*, meaning "only, alone." Monism is therefore understood as the worldview that makes everything dependent on a single absolute cause, which it calls "God."

Pantheism

46. What does the word "pantheism" then mean?

"Pantheism" derives from the Greek *pan* (all) and *theos* (God). It is used to refer to the worldview that teaches the ontological identity—that is, essential equivalence—of the phenomena of the world and the cause[3] on which these phenomena depend.

47. Can one describe pantheism by saying that it holds everything to be God?

No, it rather says that the *being* of everything is God. Not all pantheists hold God to be the totality of phenomena, but they understand Him to be the common, undivided being of the phenomena, apart from which these divided phenomena actually have no being.

48. How many forms of pantheism can you distinguish?

1. The pantheism that attempts to combine the attributes of mind and matter, of thought and extension, into a higher unity elevated above all contradiction—not as mind or matter, but as a third [entity] that we cannot conceive, but is posited as an absolute which is identical with itself.

2. The pantheism that locates the being of all things, and thus the absolute, in matter, and understands all mental phenomena as attributes and manifestations of a material substance.

3. The pantheism that locates the being of the absolute in mind and understands the material side of the world as something unreal, that is, a creation of mental representation.

---

2. V and A: "monism" (*monism*); DG: "monotheism" (*Monotheisme*).

3. DG and V: "the cause" (*de oorzaak*); A: "the absolute cause" (*de absolute oorzaak*).

The first can be called "pantheism of identity," the second "materialist pantheism," and the third "idealistic pantheism."

49. Who first used the term "pantheism"?
The deist Toland, in 1705. He called himself a "pantheist" in the title of a work on Socinianism.[4] Later on, the term "pantheism" even appeared in Faye's *Defensio religionis necnon Mosis et gentis Judaicae,* written against Toland.[5]

50. What are the main principles that all pantheists share?

1. There is no dualism in the universe, all duality of substance is rejected. There is only a *single* substance. Pantheists may consider everything to be matter, or spirit, or may even turn it into a third [entity] elevated above both. So too they may speak either of God as the world, or conversely of the world as God. Regardless, all pantheists hold there to be no distinction in essence; matter and mind, God and world, are one, identical. Not only can the world not be without God, but God also cannot be without the world. This furthermore implies that there can be no such thing as creation, unless one understands it to mean the world's development out of God from eternity through a necessary process.

2. God cannot be self-conscious or personal, except insofar as self-consciousness is one of the phenomena in which the absolute manifests itself and which therefore cannot belong to the essence. The pantheistic God is the absolute which admits of no distinction. He is not just in everything, but He is *all*; a personal being, so they say, cannot be *all,* since personality entails knowing oneself to be distinct from something else. Personalities are always distinct. Therefore, if the *all-being* were as such already personal, it would be

4. [John Toland], *Socinianism Truly Stated; Being an Example of Fair Dealing in All Theological Contversys. To Which Is Prefixt, Indifference in Disputes: Recommended by a Pantheist to an Orthodox Friend* (n.p.: London, 1705).

5. Jacques de la Faye, *Defensio religionis, necnon Mosis et gentis Judaïcae, contra duas dissertationes Joh. Tolandi* (Utrecht: Guilielmus Broed, 1709).

distinct from individual human personality and therefore not be *all*.

3. Human personality is simply a passing phenomenon in which there is no being or existence. Man before God is like a wave on the surface of the sea before the mass of waters. There is, therefore, no immortality. And there is fundamentally no moral freedom, since the *all-being* (which determines our moral acts) is actually its only cause, while our own will, our own character, are once again mere phenomena which do not operate spontaneously from themselves.
4. In all forms of pantheism, the notion of sin has the following two notable characteristics:
   a. That sin, considered as a phenomenon, is turned into something unreal, and that being (which reveals itself necessarily also in sin) is considered to be sinless, or rather elevated above all sin.
   b. That sin, as a phenomenon, is preferably still seen as something negative, as a privation of something real. Whatever is real, is power, possession in the good; and the more power and reality, the more good. This is why egotism is the principle of pantheistic ethics. For it is Godself who is powerful in the powerful person, and egotistical in the egotist, and there is nothing outside of Him to which one might appeal against Him. Whatever is, is as such good.
5. God comes to self-consciousness in humankind, comes to know Himself in it. To this degree one can say that man is the highest form of the revelation of the divinity, indeed, is Godself.

51. *What are the motives from which a pantheistic worldview can originate?*

1. Rationalism: Rationalism admits as known only what it can understand. To understand means to derive from a higher principle. According to rationalism, everything must be derived from the same principle in which everything exists. In the end, everything must be derived from a single principle. Rationalism therefore means:

a. Everything must be understood.
b. Everything must be understood from a single principle.
c. Everything must be understood from its cause, if it is to be understood [at all].
d. The human mind must be one with the world, if its laws are to depict the world laws, [if] its understanding and deduction are to depict the world system. Therefore, the very essence of rationalism is the identification of understanding and knowledge, of mental forms and its laws,[6] and that is why it leads directly to pantheism.

2. Mysticism: Mysticism seeks knowledge of the truth through an immediate intuition, an inner vision, a mystical unity with the origin of all being, with God. Pantheism is the theory that was developed to account for the illusion that is mysticism. In Spinoza, rationalism was accompanied by mysticism, turning him into a pantheist. Historically this pantheistic mysticism finds its origin in the philosophy of Plato. Plato called *Eros* the origin of all philosophy. Eros is a mythical figure by which Plato understands the pursuit of the mortal and finite for the eternal and infinite. This Eros, however, comes from Godself. Here we thus already encounter the pantheistic-mystical notion that the human race's pursuit of God has its origin in human participation in God. At first this pantheism may have restricted itself to the human soul, but later it also extended itself increasingly to the external world. This was the well from which the German mystics of the Middle Ages drew for their pantheism.

3. The pantheism of Fichte, Schelling, and Hegel had its origins in a response to the negative, skeptical results of Kant's *Critique* and in the study of Spinoza. Kant had taught that humankind can only know phenomena; since humankind and things are two, the things must always enter the human

6. DG and A: "mental forms and its laws" (*denkvormen en zijne wetten*); V: "mental capacity and its laws" (*denkverm.* [= abbr. for *denkvermogen*] *en zijne wetten*). The sense of this clause is somewhat opaque.

consciousness, that is, become phenomena before they can be known. But once the claim was made that humankind and things are not really two but one, the problem was resolved once for all. For people were now thought to know in things only their own being, and the laws that they follow and apply in that knowledge are now not just subjective laws of their mind, but also objective laws of the world. It must be observed, however, that the Spinozism of that newer philosophy no longer was the old abstract-geometrical Spinozism, but a vitalist pantheism that replaced dead substance with the living, divine, albeit not self-conscious power. As Schleiermacher put it: "No death in pantheism!"[7]

4. There is also a naturalistic pantheism. Its origins lie not so much in philosophical speculation as in the innate drive within human nature to venerate something outside itself. When true knowledge and veneration of God were lost through sin, the human race exchanged God for nature. The powers of nature were divinized; but nature is in the end one being, and so the notion took shape of a single power of nature—that is, the pantheistic God. People therefore stood still at the totality of phenomena, without ascending to a personal God as ⸢the underlying taskmaster and ruler.⸣[8]

52. *How would you criticize pantheism?*

1. Pantheism places an absolute emphasis on the primary unity and absoluteness of God and on His elevation above all division and contradiction. But as a result, it can no longer explain how the many came from the one, the finite from the absolute. If this development were a necessary one, the many and individual[9] would initially have had to be comprehended in the one and absolute—as such, its

7. Unidentified quote, which in its Dutch form as cited here also has a rather odd grammatical form: *De dood moet uit het Pantheïsme uit* (V and A); *De dood moet uit Pantheïsme uit* (DG).

8. So DG and V; omitted in A (which is therefore incomplete here).

9. V and A: "individual" (*individuele*); DG erroneously reads: "absolute" (*absolute*).

absoluteness and infinity[10] are dissolved. But if this development were free,[11] that development would become equally incomprehensible and the absoluteness would once again be lost, since one cannot conceive of freedom without personality. At the end of the day, the parts of pantheism—i.e., 1. God's absoluteness and simplicity; 2. God's necessity and self-development—conflict and cannot be reconciled. In our worldview, there is room for the former but not the latter.

2. Pantheism also does not satisfy its own rational motives from a historical perspective. The problem was to [try to] derive the multiplicity of phenomena from something simple, and to do it in such a way as to demonstrate that those phenomena, and those phenomena alone, were possible and had to come about. There is no pantheistic system that satisfies this demand. Both Spinoza and Hegel take recourse in experience for deducing the attributes of the absolute. The reason for this is that the naturalistic derivation of attributes from the absolute would introduce those attributes into the absolute, that is, resolve its simplicity.

3. It can thus be shown that pantheism's method cannot be applied consistently, that its every application must fail. But pantheism stands or falls by its method. If the human mind were the self-conscious manifestation of the absolute, it would also have to understand everything that is in the absolute, that is, it would have to be able to deduce the world, since the absolute knows itself in it. Conversely, if man is unable to demonstrate the world, then the absolute also does not know itself in him—and so pantheism is untenable. For theism the situation is altogether different, of course. It holds the world to be (1) distinct from God; (2) not necessary, but to have arisen through the free will ⸢of God⸣;[12] (3) one of the many possible worlds. Even if we cannot show why God created this world, our theism continues to stand

10. V and A: "infinity" (*onbeperktheid*); DG erroneously reads: "finitude" (*beperktheid*).

11. V and A: "free" (*vrije*); DG erroneously reads: "wise" (*wijze*).

12. So DG and V; omitted in A.

unharmed. But pantheism falls by its own method, since it teaches that the world's development is [a] development that is necessarily—on the rational level—understandable for God (= man).

4. Specifically, one can show that the various logical processes by which deduction is possible are insufficient for explaining the absolute's relationship to the finite and dependent. The relationship between the generic[13] and the individual is only an abstraction[14] of our thinking; the relationship between cause and effect is entirely universal, but can gain a specific significance for us through experience. The relationship between the whole and its parts also does not suit the pantheistic notion of the absolute if that relationship is conceived in terms of generic and individual. Finally, the principle of contradiction or negativity, which plays such an important role in the method of modern pantheistic systems, is once again an entirely logical principle which one may not take to represent a metaphysical power.

5. The normal way for people to arrive at a pantheistic notion of God is, like Spinoza, to turn the logical abstraction of substance into a metaphysical being that must then be the same in everything. We observe by way of criticism:
   a. A substance does exist in all things, that is, there is a being underlying phenomena.
   b. The fact that we give this being the one name "substance" everywhere only means that it has the same relationship to the phenomena everywhere, not that it is metaphysically the same everywhere.
   c. Pantheism makes the error of seeking to derive from the ⌜logically⌝[15] wider but metaphysically poorer concept of universal power the metaphysically richer notion of conscious, vital power. This is not possible, since the

13. V and A: "generic" (*generische*); DG erroneously reads: "faked" (*geveinste*).
14. V and DG: "abstraction" (*abstractie*); A erroneously reads: "absolution" (*absolutie*).
15. So V and A; omitted in DG.

reality of our knowledge clearly does not lend itself to such derivation.

53. How did pantheism recommend itself to many people?
By its emphasis on the unity of the world plan and on the immanence of God (against deism). However, it sacrificed God's freedom[16] and His transcendence to these two motifs, [and] identified God and world.

Deism

54. How would you describe deism?
It is a form of rationalism that, in order to maintain the exclusive right of reason as a natural source for knowledge of God, disputes the possibility of a divine revelation outside nature, thereby fundamentally abolishing the immanence of God. [According to deism,] God has created the world, endowed it with all its powers and the laws of their operation, and now leaves it to its own lot. All that He has revealed of Himself to humankind therefore consists in what already belongs to humankind by nature, created in them when they were made. Intervention by God is metaphysically or rationally[17] impossible, since it presumes that God's original work of creation was imperfect and required repair, making God imperfect.

55. What is the main objection to a deistic worldview?
That it turns religion into something superficial and universal that is calculated only for the natural state of humankind as it was fixed once and for all. If religion were just innate, it would be true only in its general contours as these contours are found in all. But then there would be no positive, no revealed religion, and also no religion of salvation. Deism thus denies the reality of sin in two ways: (a) by assuming that human nature still has sufficient knowledge of God to be able to serve Him in an upright manner; (b) by assuming that there really is no need for

---

16. DG and A: "freedom" (*vrijheid*); V: "wisdom" (*wijsheid*).
17. V and A: "rationally" (*redelijk*); DG: "morally" (*zedelijk*).

revelation, and thus for salvation. Deistic religion usually reduces itself to morality.

56. What arguments can be applied to refute it?

1. One could maintain the possibility of a supernatural revelation:
   a. From the testimony of our moral nature. God testifies through our conscience that He continually involves Himself in our affairs.
   b. From the testimony of reason, which teaches that one achieves a more elevated concept of God if He is thought of immanently rather than in purely transcendental terms.
   c. From the testimony of history. All peoples have always believed in a positive revelation from God.
2. One could demonstrate the necessity of a supernatural revelation:
   a. Every person feels the need for it, both theoretically and practically.
   b. That need has never been satisfied in any other way, also not deistically.
   c. Even if philosophy were to offer an answer to these important theoretical or practical questions, the common people who cannot practice philosophy would still need revelation.
3. One could demonstrate the reality of a supernatural revelation.

Monotheism or Theism

57. How would you define "theism" or "monotheism" in the narrower sense?
It is the teaching of a God distinct from the world and personal, the creator, sustainer, and ruler of the world. Theism includes the following elements:

1. An infinite, personal creator of all things that have dependent existence = God

2. A finite,[18] personal continuing (= immortal) I = humankind
3. A totality of objective phenomena = world

Theism holds the latter two to stand in a position of dependence on God, rather than being identical with God in the pantheistic sense.

Pluralism

58. How would you define pluralism?
It is the theory that accepts the necessary existence of more than one divine principle.

Dualism[19]

59. How many kinds of dualism are there?

1. A purely metaphysical dualism.
2. A metaphysical dualism that also bears an ethical character.

60. What do you reckon among the first class?
The various forms of hylozoism. "Hylozoism," deriving from *hylo* (matter) and *zoe* (life), is the teaching that matter is animated with life—albeit not in the materialist[20] sense, but rather such that matter and life, although distinct, still can never exist separate from each other.

61. Where did this hylozoism manifest itself in ancient philosophy?
In particular with the Stoics and their doctrine of the world soul.

62. What is the defining difference between pantheism and hylozoism?
That the latter, maintaining the distinction between matter and mind,

18. V and A: "finite" (*eindig*); DG erroneously reads: "infinite" (*oneindig*).

19. In DG the discussion of polytheism (QQ. 59–63) precedes that of dualism (QQ. 64–68). I retain the order in V and A (dualism, QQ. 59–63; polytheism, QQ. 64–68), as announced in Q. 44 according to the unanimous ms. witness.

20. DG and A: "materialistic" (*materialistische*); V: "material" (*materieele*).

can also retain the personal, continued existence[21] and immortality of the soul, together with the consciousness of the world soul.

63. What is particular to all ethical dualism?

From the opposition between two metaphysically different principles it derives the ethical opposition between good and evil, thereby raising the latter to an eternal and necessary [principle]. This ethical dualism can be found in Parsiism and in gnostic systems.

Polytheism

64. How would you define polytheism?

It is the theory that accepts the existence of more than one personal God. Polytheism is more a popular view than a scientific theory. In most cases, it seems to have originated from a personification and divinization of the powers of nature. Later on, polytheism passed into pantheism, especially among the more developed and civilized pagans, as witnessed in the development of ancient Indian Vedism into Brahmanism and Buddhism.

65. How can polytheism be further divided?

1. Fetishism (physiolatry): the worship of inorganic natural beings as it is found among many barbaric peoples
2. Zoolatry: the worship of animals, for example among the ancient Egyptians
3. Anthropomorphic polytheism: the worship of divine beings conceived in human form, for example among the Greeks and Romans

66. How does Scripture express itself on the reality of the pagan gods?

That they do not exist as gods, cannot save, etc. That belief in their existence is nevertheless a direct work of demonic powers, so that we cannot deny them all objective reality (1 Cor. 10:20).

---

21. DG: "existence" (*voortbestaan*); V and A erroneously read: "proposal" (*voorstel*).

67. What can we conclude from the universal spread of polytheism?
That it exercises a powerful appeal upon fallen human nature.

68. How is it distinguished from pantheism?
It is much less philosophically based than pantheism, and therefore cannot hold its own in the face of civilization's progress. All the same, it can offer powerful resistance against the advance of Christian culture. It has never managed to fashion an elevated ethical ideal.

Atheism

69. How many kinds of atheism can you distinguish?

1. Atheistic indifferentism, which is of a skeptical nature.
2. Materialist atheism, whose worldview leaves no place for God.

70. How many forms can atheistic indifferentism assume?

1. It can positively claim that it knows that no God exists. ⸢Then it takes the name of "dogmatic indifferentism," and rests on the absurd claim that it has investigated not only all actual, but also all possible [proofs] for the existence of God, and found them wanting.⸣[22]

22. I have reconstructed the text here to read as follows:

> Dan heet het dogmatisch Indifferentisme, en berust op de absurde beweering, dat men niet alleen alle werkelijke maar ook alle mogelijke bewijzen voor 't bestaan van God onderzocht en onvoldoende bevonden heeft.

The overall structure of the reading comes from DG, which nevertheless contains several smaller errors which I have corrected on the basis of V (and A). DG reads:

> Dan heet het dogmatisch Indifferentisme, en berust op de absurde beweering, dat men niet alleen al 't werkelijke maar ook mogelijke voor 't bestaan van 't bestaan van God onderzocht en onvoldoende bevonden heeft.

V (and, with minor variation, A) reads:

> Dat heel het Dogmatisch Indifferentisme berust op de bewering, dat men niet alleen elke werkelijke maar ook alle mogelijke bewijzen voor het bestaan van God onderzocht en onvoldoende bevonden heeft.

2. It can refrain from the positive claim that there is no God, and simply claim that there is insufficient evidence for the existence of God or for certain elements of the concept of God. For example:

    a. Like agnosticism, it can fundamentally deny humankind the ability to know the supernatural or the essence of things. To convince such agnostic atheists, one must show them that they cannot stop at this semiskeptical position, but must surrender also all knowledge of the natural and of phenomena.

    b. Like pantheism, dualism, materialism, etc., it can deny certain elements of the concept of God, such that anyone who is not a theist[23]—i.e., whoever does not do justice to the theistic concept of God—becomes an atheist. This use of the term ["atheism"] can be demonstrated historically. Cicero already referred to those who do believe in gods, yet without worshiping them and rather despising them, as atheists. The pagans later called the *Christians* atheists, since they did not recognize the pagan gods. Conversely, Christians qualified those who did away with the theistic concept of God as atheists.

71. How are we to answer the question whether atheists really do exist?
In this way, that:

1. absolutely dogmatic, positive atheism is an impossibility, a delusion, at which one can only arrive by proud self-blinding[24] and by superficiality, but that the witness of the conscience to God's existence—just like all other innate knowledge of God—remains in the deepest recesses of the heart, so that one cannot fully withdraw from it in practical life.

23. DG: "theist" (*theist*); V and A: "the first/former" (*de eerste*).

24. V and A: "self-blinding" (*zelfverblinding*); DG: "self-seduction" (*zelfverleiding*).

2. The same holds true for ⸢relative,⸣[25] negative, skeptical atheism, as well as the pantheistic, dualistic, and materialistic distortion of the notion of God. In unconscious life, the principle of faith in God remains, together with faith in those elements of the concept of God that one seems to deny, so as to be reawakened whenever the opportunity presents itself. Something innate can never be lost altogether.

72. List the traits of current materialistic atheism.

Modern materialism[26] is synonymous with evolutionism and teaches the following:

1. That energy or power[27] and matter cannot be derived[28] from each other, regardless of whether[29] one conceives of them as accompanying each other or else conceives of matter as a manifestation of energy.
2. That the physical powers of nature are the origin from which all that exists in the world came into existence so as to develop according to fixed laws. Moreover, that these physical energies, such as light, heat, electricity, magnetism, etc., can be converted into one another, demonstrating that they are only manifestations of one and the same basic energy. This final law is called the law of the conversion of energy. Some call this general basic energy "motion."
3. When these physical energies are converted into one another, this happens according to a fixed law of quantity—that is, X amount of motion produces Y amount of heat, and when that heat is reconverted, it produces the original amount of motion.

---

25. Omitted in DG.

26. DG and A: "materialism" (*materialisme*); V: "atheism" (*atheïsme*).

27. My phrase "power or energy" translates the single Dutch term *kracht*. The choice for this translation here serves to indicate that *kracht* encompasses the meaning of the two English words "power" (as in "powers of nature") and "energy" (as the term more common to modern physics).

28. DG: "derived" (*afgeleid*); V and A: "distinguished" (*afgescheiden*).

29. DG and A: "regardless of whether" (*hetzij*); V: "unless" (*tenzij*).

4. Energy is indestructible. It cannot be increased or decreased, but is eternal. This is called the law of conservation of energy, that is, the persistence of energy.
5. Therefore, life energy is nothing but a converted physical energy, and mental energy nothing but converted life energy.

73. What is the distinction between this theory and the popular materialistic theory?

According to popular materialism, everything is matter, and whatever does not appear to be matter to us, is only the operation of matter. Here the nonmaterial is thus reduced to the material. According to the evolution theory, however, matter along with all other existing things in the world are the manifestation of an unknown energy. Accordingly, to defend themselves against the charge of materialism, the proponents of this system claim that they have not reduced everything to matter, but conversely elevated matter to something immaterial, that is, to energy. While this must be granted them, the fact remains that they have lowered the mental—not, indeed, to matter, but to a blind energy that is as such no longer mental in nature.

74. How would you further criticize this system?

1. We must admit that there is continuity between the various kingdoms and classes in creation. The organic rests on the foundation of the inorganic, and in just the same way the rational[30] rests on the foundation of the organic. The evolutionists are right to the degree that they claim that the one develops from the other. However, they are wrong when they claim that there is in the organic nothing but the inorganic. Rather, in the organic there is the inorganic plus something new. In the moral,[31] there is the organic plus something new,

30. DG: "rational" (*redelijke*); V and A: "moral" (*zedelijke*).

31. V and A actually read "moral" (*zedelijke*) here; given the omission of this phrase in DG (see n. 32 below), the reading "rational" (*redelijke*) has been inserted on the basis of the general preference for DG over V and A on the choice between the terms "moral" and "rational" (see, e.g., n. 30 above, and nn. 34 and 35 below).

etc.[32] The "new" is something for which the theory of evolution has no explanation.

2. The theories that do not attempt to explain matter as a manifestation of energy, but rather understand matter and energy as two distinct, albeit related phenomena, incur the following problems:
   a. In their worldview they are just as dualistic as we are, and they are therefore actually not[33] consistently materialistic.
   b. They cannot account for the foundation on which the specific connection between these two principles of matter and energy rests. If they are mutually independent, how can each on its own be absolutely necessary?

3. The law of the conversion of energy has not been proved. According to its proponents, it rests on the following arguments:
   a. Just like the joining of two chemical elements (e.g., hydrogen and oxygen) produces a new substance with new properties (i.e., water), one must analogously account for the origin of life and rationality[34] from a joining of two or more non⌜rational⌝[35] and nonliving elements. They claim that the latter is no more incomprehensible than the former. While this may be true on the level of incomprehensibility, there still is a big difference separating these two cases. What comes from oxygen and hydrogen may well have properties that differ from the properties of the two original elements, and yet they are properties that remain the same on the level of species—that is, they are material properties. What the proponents of this theory would have us believe,

32. So V and A; DG erroneously reads: "The *in*organic + something new = the rational. The organic + something new etc. etc." (*Het* an*organische* + *iets nieuws* = *'t redelijke. Het organische* + *iets nieuws enz. enz.*).

33. So DG and A; the negative is erroneously omitted in V.

34. DG: "rationality" (*redelijkheid*); V and A: "morality" (*zedelijkheid*).

35. DG and V: "rational" (*redelijke*); A: "moral" (*zedelijke*).

however, is that the joining of two of more lifeless[36] elements can produce properties differing on the level of genus or species—namely, something living and moral. This, however, is altogether impossible.

b. It is thought that there are direct proofs for the conversion of normal mechanical energies [or powers] into organic powers at work in the body—in other words, that a vital heat is no different from normal, natural heat in lifeless objects. We would respond that, even if it could be demonstrated that the energies in the body of an organic being are found also in inorganic nature, this still does not explain how the organic bond and the interlocking of these energies in the organism come about.

4. There is an absolute divide between the physical mechanism and sensible life. There is no correspondence whatsoever between the motion of atoms and sensation. To this end, the theory of energy must remain standing, since the divide between matter and sensation is no greater than the divide between blind energy and sensation.

5. When some accept that mute motion can be explained, but sensible life cannot and will not ever be explained, while still maintaining that there must be a certain relationship [between them] such that sensation is to be conceived as arising from the motion of atoms, their reasoning is altogether false. The final claim could only be maintained if this arising were thought to have an explanation, or at the very least the possibility of an explanation in the future. Since this is not so, the claim makes no sense at all. If the unity exists, it cannot[37] be held to be *a priori* inexplicable; ⌜and if it is *a priori* held to be inexplicable,⌝[38] this amounts to an admission that it does not exist.

---

36. So V and A; DG adds: "or irrational" (*of redelooze*).
37. DG: "cannot" (*kan zij niet*); V and A erroneously drop the negative (*niet*).
38. So DG and V; erroneously omitted in A.

II. A Critical Overview of the Various Theories That Seek to Explain the Origin and Development of Religion

75. How many theories are there to explain the rise of the concept of God among human beings?
Four: 1. The theory of development. 2. The theory of revelation. 3. The theory of inference. 4. The theory of intuition.

The Theory of Development

76. What does the first theory—i.e., the theory of development—teach?
That the concept of God in general, and the monotheistic concept of God in particular, is the product of a long developmental process, in which it gradually took shape from totally different factors of a nonreligious nature. It thus teaches that the concept of God is not original, but derived.

77. What theories must be mentioned here?[39]

1. The theory of Hume: According to him, there first were many gods, and polytheism ruled the day.[40] Through accidental, largely local circumstances one God then came to be venerated more than the others, until the others receded into the background and only a single one remained. This is how monotheism arose. This theory condemns itself, since it must take refuge in something accidental for its explanation.
2. Comte's theory, also called "fetishistic"—not because he coined the name "fetish," but because he first defended the theory that all religion originated in or began with fetishism.[41] The name "fetish" was first used by the French author De Brosses in 1760.[42] Portuguese seafarers saw the indigenous

39. Cf. Francis L. Patton, *Notes from Lectures on Theistic Conception of the Universe* (Princeton: n.p., 1883), 4–11.

40. David Hume, *The Natural History of Religion* (1757; London: A. and H. Bradlaugh Bonner, 1889).

41. Auguste Comte, *The Catechism of Positive Religion*, trans. Richard Congreve, 2nd ed. (London: Trübner, 1883), 255–69; cf. John Stuart Mill, *The Positive Philosophy of Auguste Comte* (Boston: William V. Spencer, 1866), 170–71.

42. Charles de Brosses, *Du Culte des Dieux Fétiches ou Parallèle de l'ancienne Religion de l'Egypte avec la Religion Actuale de Nigritie* (1760); Rosalind C. Morris and Daniel H.

peoples on the coast of Africa venerate such objects as their amulets or rosaries, and gave this religion the name *fetices*, since they gave their sacred objects the Portuguese name *feitiço* (magic),[43] derived from the Latin *factitius*.[44] A fetish is a tangible, palm-sized, lifeless object which is religiously venerated or, in its metaphorical wider sense, anything that is venerated in a superstitious manner (e.g., the Bible). The reasons for which fetishism is called the oldest form of religion are as follows:

a. It is the lowest form of religion.
b. It is the religion of the majority of uncivilized nations today. These barbaric nations, so it is thought, can be considered types of the original human race.
c. Empiric philosophy seeks to explain the rise of religion using the theory of developments, and thinks it can begin with fetishism.

In criticism of this theory we offer the following remarks:

a. Not all evolutionists accept this theory. It is rejected by H. Spencer, as well as Max Müller and Pfleiderer.[45]
b. When one indeed encounters fetishistic worship, it is most difficult to determine whether this fetish is only the specific manifestation of a general conception of God, or whether the fetish itself is taken to be God. The former seems most likely, meaning that another concept of God lies hidden beneath the fetishistic worship.
c. Nations that have been ensnared by fetishism could also have fallen down to it from a higher level of religion. There is no evidence suggesting that fetishism is the original form.
d. Before a fetishistic worshiper imagines a stick, cloth, or

---

Leonard, *The Returns of Fetishism: Charles de Brosses and the Afterlives of an Idea. With a New Translation of* On the Worship of Fetish Gods (Chicago: University of Chicago Press, 2017).

43. V: *feitico* (*feitisao = toverij*); A: *feitico*; DG: *feitizo*.

44. DG: *factitius*; V and A erroneously read: *factitium*.

45. DG: *Pfleiderer*; V and A erroneously read: *Pfeidler*.

the like to be animated with life, he must already have had a general concept of a living power, meaning that fetishism is indeed not the first thing representing his point of departure.

3. Herbert Spencer's theory, according to which all religion has arisen from ancestor worship.[46] Spencer lists the following stages of development:
   a. Through dreams, people come to the concept of a soul distinct from the body.
   b. They conclude from this that the soul also continues to exist when the body is dissolved.
   c. That the souls of the dead therefore continually demand a display of love and veneration.
   d. Later the religion of ancestor worship passed into other forms of fetishism like the worship of animals, etc.

Our criticism on this theory runs as follows:

   a. It is only one of the many ways in which religion could have arisen, but this hypothesis does not amount to proof that it really did arise this way.
   b. Spencer has failed to demonstrate that when people were worshiping their ancestors, they at that time did not worship gods distinct from their ancestors. According to the Vedas, the two appear to have gone together.[47]
   c. Spencer has similarly failed to demonstrate that there is no essential difference between the sense of reverence that one feels for one's ancestors or parents and the sense of awe we feel for the divinity that we call "religion."
   d. The fact that the savage considers God as his father may not be used to assume that all religion originally took the form of ancestor worship. If that were the case, one might

46. Herbert Spencer, *The Principles of Sociology*, 3rd ed. (1876; New York: D. Appleton, 1921), 1:285–305.

47. In A, point b is still part of the first point of criticism, meaning that it lists a total of only five points.

just as well conclude from the "Our Father" [of the Lord's Prayer] that Christians worship an ancestor in their God.

e. The proof of explanation[48] which Spencer has given to account for the rise of other forms of religion from ancestor worship is most artificial and indeed unsatisfying.

f. Spencer has failed to find an answer to the objection against his theory charging that one finds ancestor worship only among the lower classes of savages, and not among the Arian (Indo-Germanic) or Semitic nations.

4. Hegel's theory is the total opposite of the theory of the evolutionists on the point of the developmental process. Spencer and others begin with atoms or energy, and from there go on to seek to explain the development of the world. Hegel begins with the idea, and from there goes on to develop the process of the world. He thus takes the opposite starting point, although in both cases religion still is the product of a development from other factors.

5. Max Müller. It is very difficult to locate the position adopted by this scholar.

   a. Against the theory of Comte, he has offered convincing proof that fetishism is not the original form of religion.

   b. In his Hibbert Lectures,[49] he distances himself somewhat from his earlier thesis of a religious instinct in the human race.[50]

   c. Although Müller has never denied that monotheism or faith in God can be the most ancient [of religions], these days he still claims that this form of religion cannot be the original one (i.e., it cannot be as old as the human race), but he argues that humanity must already have completed

48. V and A: "the proof of explanation" (*proeve van [A:* der*] verklaring*); DG: "processes of explanation" (*processen van verklaring*).

49. DG: "Hibbert Lectures" (*Hibbert Lectures*); A: "[blank] lexicon" (*lexicon*); V: "[blank] lexicon," and in the margin, "Hibbert lectures" (*lexicon;* margin: *Hibbert lectures*).

50. F. Max Müller, *Lectures on the Origin and Growth of Religion: As Illustrated by the Religions of India* (London: Longmans, Green, 1878).

half of its course before it reaches this stage. For the thesis that monotheism is as old as the human race, one therefore cannot appeal to Max Müller.

Theory of Revelation

78. What must be observed in regard to the second theory on the origin of religion?

1. One must draw a distinction between revelation and tradition. The question is not how we come to believe in God, but how, in general, the first faith in God came to be in the human race.
2. One must draw a distinction between the purifying and illuminating influence of the revelation of the Bible on theism,[51] and the role that revelation originally had for the rise[52] of theism.
3. Sharply formulated, the question is therefore whether one must ascribe the rise of the first theism to revelation.

79. How have some sought to explain the theistic sentiments that one finds in pagan philosophy?

People have tried to derive them from the contact into which the pagan world came with the Jews.

80. What must be observed in regard to this, and in general in regard to this theory of revelation?

1. If the human race had been altogether deprived of an innate concept of God, revelation could not have communicated it to them.
2. A form of polytheism mingled with theistic elements already existed long before the pagan world came into contact with the Jews. Now one either has the option of saying that these theistic elements are remnants of an earlier revelation given

---

51. DG: "on theism" (*op het Theisme*); V and A: "or of theism" (*of het Theisme*).
52. DG: "rise" (*teweegbrengen*); V and A: "return" (*terugbrengen*).

before the division of the nations, or else insisting that they developed from that innate concept of God. Yet there no longer is any ground to deny that also a purer theism can develop from there.

3. There is no proof suggesting that tradition alone can achieve or maintain such a ⸢general⸣[53] phenomenon as faith in God. A general fact requires a general cause, and tradition happens to be accidental and particular. For religion in general we must appeal to something other than revelation and tradition. Why would this not apply to theism as well?
4. All tradition does not necessarily go back to revelation. It can pass on what in the prefall state was the natural voice of the human mind, but in the current sinful state requires the aid and influence of tradition to survive.

Theory of Inference

81. What does the third theory teach?

That humankind arrives at knowledge of God by a logical process of inference.

82. Can this theory be adopted in different forms?

One could say either that all human religion has been acquired by way of inference, or that the foundation of religion rests on intuition (innate knowledge), but that theism must develop from there through inference. ⸢The former position is more consistent.⸣[54]

83. Do some speak also of unconscious inference?

Yes, but it is not very clear what they mean by it, since inference and unconsciousness seem to be mutually exclusive.

84. What follows from our thesis regarding the scientific defensibility and maintainability of theism?

That also the possibility of its rise by inference cannot be denied. History

53. So DG and A; omitted in V.

54. So V and A; omitted in DG.

teaches us that theism developed here and there from polytheism using scientific means (Plato, Aristotle), but in general people first believed in God and only then began to draw inferences.

Theory of Intuition

85. What does the fourth theory teach about the rise of religion?
That it depends on intuition, that is, on a principle for knowledge of God innate to the human mind which does need a connection with the outer world in order to develop, but is conversely also absolutely necessary for our connection with the outer world in order to lead to knowledge of God.

86. What unites all the theories that we classify in this category?
The thesis that faith in God does not owe its origin to objective revelation or conscious[55] inference, but that it, resting on intuition (understood in the widest possible sense), precedes all revelation and reasoning.

87. What was the view of Schelling and Cousin on this point?
They accepted the presence of an immediate knowledge of God (i.e., of the absolute) in the human race.[56]

88. What did Jacobi and Schleiermacher teach?[57]
They pointed to emotion as the origin of knowledge of God or religion. Although this theory expresses a positive response to the entirely moralistic concept of religion in Kant and others, it still remained a one-sided and dangerous endeavor to call that emotion an awareness of God, and to confuse emotion and awareness so as to appear to exclude all knowledge from religion.

55. DG and A: "conscious" (*bewuste*); V erroneously reads: "unconscious" (*onbewuste*).

56. F. W. J. Schelling, *System of Transcendental Idealism* (Charlottesville: University Press of Virginia, 1997); Victor Cousin, *Premiers essais de philosophie*, 3rd ed. (Paris: Librairie nouvelle, 1855).

57. Cf. Isaac Dorner, *System of Christian Doctrine* (Edinburgh: T&T Clark, 1880), 1:208; Francis L. Patton, "The Origin of Theism," *The Presbyterian Review* 3, no. 12 (1882): 732–60.

89. Describe Calderwood's view.

He is of the opinion that faith in an infinite God is a necessary, innate faith, but he is also convinced that all proofs for the existence of God fall short.[58] This is somewhat dangerous, since it makes the truth of the concept of God depend on its intuitive character.

90. How does Charles Hodge express himself on the matter?

He, too, holds the idea of God to be innate. (1) He maintains the validity of the proofs for the existence of God. (2) He does not identify this innate idea of God with the true, theistic idea of God; to his mind, it is much more general and less pure. (3) He has this idea of God precede all conscious inference.[59]

91. What emerges from these different views on the meaning of the word "intuition"?

That it has a very vague and unspecified range of meaning. "Intuition" can be understood as: (1) An immediate knowledge of God in a pantheistic or semipantheistic sense, following Schelling and Cousin. The human race possesses no such knowledge. (2) An in itself clear and logically formulated judgment. That is not what our faith in God is. (3) An innate inclination of our mind to come to faith in God. It is a kind of principle or predisposition to faith in God. Most of those who speak of an idea of God through intuition connect it to this view. Nevertheless, this idea, too, allows for different formulations, such as:

1. The view that innate knowledge of God is like a kind of quick and semi-unconscious inference of the kind we make when we recognize an ⸢old⸣[60] friend, for example. This is the view to which Charles Hodge seems to be inclined.

58. Henry Calderwood, *Philosophy of the Infinite: A Treatise on Man's Knowledge of the Infinite Being in Answer to Sir William Hamilton and Dean Mansel*, 3rd ed. (London: Macmillan, 1872).

59. Charles Hodge, *Systematic Theology* (New York: Scribner, Armstrong, 1873), 1:192–95.

60. So V and A; omitted in DG.

2. The view that the idea of God is the self-given correlate to the idea of the infinite.[61] This is the view of Cousin.
3. The view of the pantheists, who teach that God comes to self-consciousness in us, such that human thinking about God is God thinking about Himself in the human being.
4. The idea of God can be considered an immediate testimony which God has given in us of His own existence. It is thus an innate idea and is produced by the Holy Spirit, specifically by the common grace of the Holy Spirit. It should, however, be emphasized that this idea is only ⸢a principle⸣[62] of knowledge of God requiring contact with the outer world and all kinds of inference in order to develop to actual knowledge of God.[63] The advantages of this view are as follows:
   a. It means we feel no need to be moved to[64] declare all objective proofs for the existence of God unnecessary.
   b. However, since the concept of God is not the product of scientific induction, it at the same time has a fixed foundation through inductive proof.
   c. This view offers the best account of all theories of innate knowledge of God.
   d. It offers a natural foundation on which the building of revelation can be erected.
   e. It leaves the possibility for Adam and his descendants to know God in the same way, at least in general.
   f. It is fully compatible with the doctrine of the immanence of God, which holds that He will also reveal Himself immediately in our mind.

61. V and A: "infinite" (*oneindige*); DG erroneously reads: "finite" (*eindige*).

62. So V and A; erroneously omitted in DG.

63. Here Vos may refer to the views of Abraham Kuyper on common grace. See Abraham Kuyper, *Principles of Sacred Theology*, trans. J. Henrik de Vries (1898; Grand Rapids: Eerdmans, 1963), 265.

64. V and A: "to" (*om*); DG erroneously reads: "from" (*van*).

III. A Discussion of the Ontological Argument

92. Who was the first to use the term "ontological argument"?
Kant, in his work *The Only Possible Argument in Support of a Demonstration of the Existence of God.*[65]

93. What does the term "ontological" mean?
"Ontological" forms a contrast with the terms "cosmic" or "psychological." An ontological proof is a proof that is not applied with respect to God's relationship to something outside of Him, but simply from the idea of God as He is in Himself.

94. Where do we find early traces of the ontological argument?
In Plato, Cleanthes the Stoic, and Diogenes Laertius. In a more developed form, it first appears in the Middle Ages. Since then, it has assumed three forms: (1) The form of Anselm. (2) That of Descartes and Spinoza. (3) The modern form since the days of Kant.

Anselm

95. What proof did Anselm first attempt to offer for the existence of God?
In his *Monologion* he attempted, in Platonic fashion, to deduce the existence of God from the idea of God. Not satisfied with this, he developed his ontological argument in the form of a prayer to God (therefore called the *Proslogion*).[66]

96. What is the main idea of the argument?
It finds expression in what Anselm says to God: "You are something greater than which nothing can be thought." But, so Anselm argues, if God were only thought and did not exist, we would be able to think of something greater—namely, an existing God. Yet that would conflict

---

65. Immanuel Kant, "The Only Possible Argument in Support of a Demonstration of the Existence of God," in *Theoretical Philosophy, 1755–1770*, ed. David Walford (Cambridge: Cambridge University Press, 1992), 107–201.

66. Anselm of Canterbury, *The Major Works*, ed. Brian Davies and G. R. Evans (Oxford: Oxford University Press, 1998).

with the basic presupposition that God is the greatest that can be thought. Therefore, God exists.

97. What is your judgment on the critique charging that Anselm's argument rests entirely on his realism?

This critique has been made by Fortlage and Hasse.[67] According to them, Anselm argues as follows: (1) What exists in our concept, exists also in reality. (2) A being greater than which nothing can be thought exists in concept. (3) Therefore, it also exists in reality. An objection to this [reading of Anselm] is that such reasoning would be left exposed to all the objections which Gaunilo, Count of Montigny, already proposed against Anselm's argument. Yet this was not how Anselm argued. He did not simply conclude the reality of the concept from the existence of the concept, claiming that the concept would otherwise be self-contradictory. He stated that his argument was entirely unique, and applicable to nothing but the most perfect being.

98. How then does Anselm's argument actually work?

He appears to assume that, once the concept of the most perfect being is recognized to be present in the mind, every contradiction must be removed from the concept. His argument is thus in its entirety a proof of concept. A concept must be developed in terms of its logical content, and from that concept (i.e., the content of the concept) its existence must be deduced—not from the presence, but from the content of the concept.

99. Where does Anselm err?

1. He does not err in his claim that "a concept may contain no contradictions." We can, for example, eliminate every element of weakness from the concept of a most perfect being.

67. Karl Fortlage, *Darstellung und Kritik der Beweise für Daseyn Gottes* (Heidelberg: Karl Groos, 1840), 131, 146; Friedrich Rudolf Hasse, *Anselm von Canterbury*, 2 vols. (Leipzig: W. Engelmann, 1843); Hasse, *The Life of Anselm, Archbishop of Canterbury*, trans. William Turner (London: Rivington, 1850); cf. F. L. Patton, review of *Historic Aspects of the* A Priori *Argument Concerning the Being and Attributes of God*, by John Gibson Cazenove, *The Presbyterian Review* 7, no. 28 (1886): 765.

2. He does, however, err (a) in that he considers the predicate of existence one of the attributes that is included in the sum of the attributes of the concept and the predicate of non-existence an attribute that cannot coexist with the other attributes of the concept. This is altogether false. A concept does not become richer or poorer depending on whether I assign or deny it existence. Our concept of a thing would fall short with respect to its reality only if we could think or imagine it without imagining it for ourselves as being or existing. But we never do that. Whatever is thought or imagined is thought or imagined as existing. Its existence is imagined along with [the concept], even though we do not thereby intend to pronounce a modality judgment on it, claiming that it really does exist. To will to think a concept in this sense without willing to think it as existing would indeed involve contradiction. It should be noted, however, that this thought or imagined way of existence[68] accrues to all concepts, and therefore could not have been what Anselm intended. (b) When we include this existence with the concept in thought or imagination, we must maintain that there is no longer a difference in magnitude between such a concept and its reality. The difference between them is of an altogether different, metaphysical nature, and resists closer description. Yet it is sufficiently clear that it is not a difference in quantity, as if we could conclude from the quantitative concept of God as the most perfect being something about the existence of God.

100. Anselm's argument also contains another proof, doesn't it?

Yes, sometimes it seems as if Anselm's argument was contracted in the following premises and conclusion:

1. The greatest being that can be thought must be thought as necessarily existing.
2. God is the greatest being that can be thought.

68. V erroneously inserts a division here: *a*).

3. Therefore, God must be thought to exist necessarily, that is, God exists.

101. What does the major [premise] in this syllogism mean?
The greatest being that we can think is a being that cannot not exist. That is certainly true—that is, the absolute is a predicate of the concept of the greatest being.

102. How does Anselm continue his reasoning?
He reasons in this way: if I were to doubt the actual existence of this greatest being, I would introduce into its concept a predicate contradicting this predicate of absoluteness.

103. What logical error is being committed here?
That my doubt or belief regarding the existence of the absolute, which merely expresses this relationship between my mind and knowledge and the absolute, is confused[69] with an internal change in the concept itself. I by definition must think the absolute as necessarily existing, ⸢but the question is whether such a necessarily existing thing⸣[70] is real.

104. Which two meanings of the term "necessary existence" are being confused here?

1. The logical or modal meaning, which expresses a relationship between a concept and my knowing mind. Something can exist necessarily for me. That is, the knowledge of the thing can be something that is necessarily established for me, even though metaphysically it is not necessary, that is, it also could not exist.

2. The metaphysical meaning, which signifies that a thing

69. A (and DG): "expresses a [DG: this] relationship between my mind and knowledge and the absolute, is confused" (*eene* [DG: *deze*] *verhouding van mijn geest en mijn kennen tot dit absolute uitdrukt, verwisseld wordt*); V erroneously reads: "is a relationship of my mind, expresses my knowledge of the absolute, is confused" (*eene verhouding van mijn geest is, mijn kennen tot dit absolute uitdrukt, verwisseld wordt*).

70. So DG and V; omitted in A (error by homoioteleuton).

has the absolute cause of its existence within itself, that it depends on nothing else. As such, a thing can be metaphysically necessary without for that reason being modally necessary to me, and vice versa.

105. How Platonic is the foundation to this argument?
It more or less proceeds from the assumption that the cause of reality which a thing has, and the degree of certainty which we have concerning the existence of that thing, are coextensive.

Descartes and Spinoza

106. What form does the ontological argument assume in Descartes?
Spinoza and Descartes, like Anselm, sought to demonstrate that the existence of God is comprehended in the concept of God, just like the sum of the angles in a triangle equaling two right angles is comprehended in the concept of a triangle.[71]

107. What is specific to Descartes's argument?
He seeks to combine the ontological and anthropological (cosmological) arguments. Kuno Fischer presents Descartes's line of reasoning as follows:[72]

1. The idea of a most perfect being is in us. Nothing can be deduced from it if that idea were not necessary for us.
2. That idea is necessary for us, but even then its reality cannot be deduced from it.
3. The idea must be considered as having been produced in us by a most perfect being, since the finite can never from itself produce the idea of the infinite. This proves the reality of the idea of God according to the law of causality.

---

71. Benedict Spinoza, *Ethics,* trans. Edwin Curley (New York: Penguin Classics, 2005), 1–31; René Descartes, *Principles of Philosophy,* in *The Philosophical Writings of Descartes,* vol. 1, trans. John Cottingham, Bert Stoothoff, Dugald Murdoch (Cambridge: Cambridge University Press, 1985), 193–222.

72. Kuno Fischer, *Descartes and His School,* trans. John P. Gordy (London: T. Fisher Unwin, 1890), 349–54.

108. What specific connection can we already detect in Descartes?
Between the rationalist notion of *ideae innatae* (innate ideas) and the ontological argument.

109. In whom does this become even clearer?
In Spinoza, who moves from the concept which we have of substance to conclude the existence of God as substance. For all things their existence is something external, but for the concept of substance its existence is essential, since it constitutes[73] the content of the concept.

Kant and Later

110. Why was Kant's critique of the proofs for God's existence so important?

1. Because it was the first attempt to classify the proofs.
2. Because it was a negative critique, which rejected all these proofs and thus exerted great influence.

111. Give a general overview of the main content of Kant's critique of these proofs.
Kant claimed[74]

1. that there are only three possible proofs of speculative reason—namely, the ontological, the cosmological, and the physico-teleological;[75]
2. that a devastating critique can be launched against each of these proofs;
3. that cosmological and physico-teleological[76] arguments can in the end be reduced to the ontological.

---

73. DG and A: "constitutes" (*uitmaakt*); V erroneously reads: "does not constitute" (*niet uitmaakt*).

74. Kant, *Critique of Pure Reason*, 578ff.; cf. Caspar Wistar Hodge Jr., *The Kantian Epistemology and Theism: A Dissertation Presented to the Faculty of Princeton College for the Degree of Doctor of Philosophy* (Philadelphia: MacCalla, 1894), 31–33.

75. DG: "physico-teleological" (*Physico-teleolog.*); V and A: "physico-theological" (*Physico-Theologisch*).

76. DG: "physico-teleological" (*ph. teleologisch*); V: "theological (teleological)" (*Theologisch (Teleologisch)*); A: "theleological" (*Theleolo.*; sic.).

112. What is Kant's specific critique on the ontological argument?

1. That the examples adduced to prove agreement between subject and object pertain only to judgments, not concepts. Thus, from the image of a triangle, as Descartes had used it, it does follow that if a triangle exists, it exists that way, but it does not follow that the triangle exists. The same applies to the idea of the most perfect being.
2. That it is absurd to include a concept's existence as a predicate in the content of that concept. That a thing exists is not an analytic but a synthetic judgment. That is, a predicate is not in the subject, but must be added to it.
3. Existence is therefore not a real predicate. If objective existence were a predicate, a concept of a thing could never correspond with the thing itself.

113. What observations must be made in regard to Kant's critique?

1. That it is valid, provided that one only seek to develop the existence of God from the concept. However, in the ontological argument we still find the expression of the idea innate in us that a necessary, absolute being exists, and how it must be thought. The ontological argument errs in that it seeks to prove what we should be accepting simply on the basis of the testimony of this idea.
2. That according to Kant himself the idea of a necessary, absolute being must inevitably be formed by us, although Kant refuses to see in this inevitability a predicate of truth.[77]
3. That Kant himself accepts the idea of the absolute (= God) again on the ground of practical reason, and on the sole ground that it is necessary for us to accept such a being.

77. A reverses the order between 2 and 3.

114. What is the position of Schelling and Hegel on the ontological argument?
They attempted to restore it to its honor, albeit in a sense matching their pantheistic philosophy.[78] Here thinking and being are, of course, one.

IV. A Discussion of the Cosmological Argument

115. What two meanings can one attach to the term "cosmological argument"?

1. The specific meaning: the argument that proceeds from the world as something accidental to the existence of something absolute.
2. The general meaning, or every argument that ascends from the world to God using the concept of causality.[79]

In this [latter] sense the teleological argument would become a part of the cosmological argument. We understand the cosmological [argument] in the former sense—namely, the argument that proceeds from the contingent existence of the world to the existence of God.

116. Is the cosmological argument old?
Yes, we already find it in Aristotle's concept of a First Mover.[80]

117. In how many forms can the cosmological argument be treated?
It can be applied

1. to the totality of the contingent phenomena of the world;
2. to specific contingent phenomena of the world.

---

78. F. W. J. Schelling, *On the History of Modern Philosophy*, trans. Andrew Bowie (Cambridge: Cambridge University Press, 1994), 87–89; G. W. F. Hegel, *The Science of Logic*, trans. George di Giovanni (Cambridge: Cambridge University Press, 2010), 45–226.

79. V and A: "causality" (*oorzakelijkheid*); DG: "necessity" (*noodzakelijkheid*).

80. Aristotle, *Metaphysics*, XII, 1072a, in *The Basic Works of Aristotle*, ed. Richard McKeon (New York: Random House, 1941).

118. What syllogism can be used to formulate it?

1. Every effect has a cause.
2. The world is an effect.
3. The world has a cause = God.

119. What objection can be raised against this argument?

To say that every effect has a cause is tautological. It only means that everything that is subject to change and transformation—that is, began to exist at some point in time—must have a cause. But one wonders whether the world really is such a thing (= an effect in this sense).

120. Can we follow Kant in denying the validity of the law of causality?[81]

No, for the result would be skepticism.

121. Can we accept the empirical view on causality as proposed by David Hume and John Stuart Mill?[82]

No, for

1. there can be regular succession where there is no causality;
2. from this opinion follows an infinite regress, an endless series of causes and effects extending both backward and forward;
3. this view, too, leads to skepticism, given that experience, which alone must decide in matters relating to succession, can never provide us with absolute truth.

122. Is it easy to prove that the world is an effect in the above sense?

No, for in that case we would have had to see how it came into existence.

123. How can it still be demonstrated?

By pointing out that there is nothing in the world that bears the

81. Kant, *Prolegomena to Any Future Metaphysics*.

82. John Stuart Mill, *Notes on the Analysis*, in *Collected Works of John Stuart Mill*, ed. John M. Robson (Toronto: University of Toronto Press, 1989), 31:161; David Hume, *A Treatise on Human Nature*, ed. David Fate Norton and Mary J. Norton (Oxford: Clarendon, 2007); Hume, *An Enquiry Concerning Human Understanding*, ed. Tom L. Beauchamp (Oxford: Clarendon, 2000).

character of an absolute (= uncaused) cause. Science today seeks to view all of world history as a process of becoming, behind which must lie an unknown cause of all these changes in form. This, too, is the core of the cosmological argument.

124. What is this argument's strength and its weakness?
Its strength lies in the fact that it points us to the necessary existence of a cause for all that comes into being.

Its weakness lies in the fact that it teaches us nothing about this cause, except that it is a cause. We do not learn whether this cause is mind, is one, works teleologically, etc. It also cannot teach us whether this cause can exist separately from the world or is inseparably tied to it. Pantheism can therefore use this argument just as well as we can; it is not specifically theistic.

125. Why can we not extend the series of causes and effects into infinity?
The reason for this does not lie in the concept of causality itself, which only demands that every effect must have a cause, but does not in any way demand the presence of an absolute cause behind all effects and causes. But the reason is rather to be found in the innate idea of something absolute which has the ground of its existence within itself and on which this world in its accidental nature rests.

126. How does Kant judge the inclination of the human mind to accept such an absolute cause?
He acknowledges the presence of this inclination in human beings, but only accords it subjective validity. According to Kant, the reason we speak of an absolute cause is that our mind would never be able to grasp or comprehend the world if there were an infinite chain of causes and effects. Since we do want [to comprehend the world], we accept as truth what we want—that is, finitude in the series of causes and effects, implying that there must be an absolute cause at the beginning.

127. How would you counter Kant's critique here?
From what Kant says, it would follow that the human mind always replaces the truth with its wishes and inclinations. This is not so,

however. At times we have to recognize as truth what is actually diametrically opposed to our inclination to comprehend everything. For example, we think of space and time as being infinite, even though that very fact also indicates the impossibility for us ever to be able to grasp it with our representation. The truth is that an infinite series [of causes] is just as unsatisfying for our understanding of causality as a finite series [of causes] is. But the innate idea of the absolute, self-existing, necessary[83] being excludes such an infinite series. It was on this innate idea that the ontological argument rested. Its error just lies in its attempt to prove rather than to show. It ought to have restricted itself to showing the existence of such an innate idea in us. It should by now be becoming clear how the ontological argument [in this] adjusted [form] naturally joins the cosmological argument, and how they are mutually complementary.

128. To which two classes of specific phenomena have people wanted to apply the cosmological argument in particular?
To phenomena of thought and to phenomena of life in general.

129. Who applied it to phenomena of thought, and how?
Locke construed the following argument: Whatever thinks, that is, is mind, can never come from something that does not think and is not mind.[84] Now in the world there is thinking and mind. They must therefore have been produced by a thinking and mental being, since they could not have been produced by anything else. Therefore, there is from eternity an ⸢eternally⸣[85] thinking, mental being = God.

130. How would you criticize this argument?
The question is whether the thought and mind existing in this world are actually a product, ⸢or have rather always been existing.⸣[86] ⸢If the former

83. DG and A: "necessary" (*noodzakelijk*); V: "infinite" (*oneindige*).

84. John Locke, *An Essay Concerning Human Understanding*, ed. Peter Nidditch (Oxford: Oxford University Press, 1975).

85. So V; omitted in DG and A.

86. So DG and V; omitted in A (error by homoioteleuton involving "existence" [*bestaan*]).

is true, Locke's argument fails.'[87] If the latter is true, one could say that the conscious, individual phenomenon which I call my mind and my thinking has arisen in time, but that they are only phenomena, while the unconscious and absolute mind that is at its foundation is eternal and not a product—in other words, Locke's argument does not reckon with the possibility of pantheism.[88] He may therefore arrive at a better conclusion than we did in our cosmological argument, but his argument hides a *petitio prinicipii*—namely, that the individually thinking[89] spirit is a product. At this point one might still ask whether there must be a cause for the conscious and individual arising from the unconscious and absolute world spirit. As such, however, the cause would be located in the latter itself. Or else the one phenomenon could cause the other. Regardless, along this line of reasoning we cannot get beyond a position common to both theism and pantheism.

131. Who has applied the cosmological argument to phenomena from life in general?
Hamilton and others.[90] They proceed from life as organic life and from there argue on a teleological basis, or else they think very specifically of rationally thinking life, making this argument equivalent to Locke's.

V. A Discussion of the Physico-Teleological Argument

132. Which two arguments can you distinguish under the name "teleological"?

1. The argument from order.
2. The argument from purpose.

---

87. So DG; erroneously omitted in V and A.

88. V and A: "pantheism" (*Pantheïsme*); DG: "Platonism" (*Platonisme*).

89. V and A: "thinking" (*denkende*); DG: "existing" (*bestaande*).

90. William Hamilton, *Philosophy of Sir William Hamilton, Bart.*, ed. O. W. Wight, 6th ed. (New York: D. Appleton, 1866), 66; cf. John Stuart Mill, *Sir William Hamilton's Philosophy and of the Principal Philosophical Questions Discussed in His Writings*, 2 vols. (New York: Henry Holt, 1873).

133. Can these two arguments be separated from each other?
No, for wherever a purpose is present, there is order. And wherever order is present, there is purpose. So, too, the core of the teleological argument is the same in both.

134. Is it logically impossible for order and purpose to originate accidentally from the coherence of blind powers?
That is a claim that cannot be made. Rather, one must demonstrate why that is unlikely.

135. Which elements must be treated in order when we consider the teleological argument?

1. The teleological reasoning itself.
2. The proofs of ⸢order and⸣[91] purpose which the world has to offer.
3. The main objections which have been offered against the teleological argument.
4. The various accounts which people have attempted to offer for the phenomena of order and purpose.

136. Is the concept of finality an intuition like the concept of causality is? That is, do we know a priori *that everything must have a purpose, just as we know* a priori *that everything that happens must have a cause?*
No, this is not the case. The teleological view on things is not simple but compound, so that we can parse it into its parts. The causal view on things is simple and cannot be reduced to more simple elements.

137. On what does the teleological argument rest?
On the principle of analogy. In the teleological argument, we reason as follows:

1. There is analogy and concord in the world. When certain phenomena are regularly accompanied by others, we

---

91. So DG and V; omitted in A.

conclude that this is so everywhere; and wherever we encounter the former phenomena, we assume the latter to be present as well, even though we do not see them. This is the major [premise].

2. Our own experience tells us that whatever we produce in a purposive and orderly manner is accompanied by a purposeful operation of our mind. When we encounter phenomena of purpose and order in the world resembling the effect of our own purpose, we assume that they are accompanied by a Purposer and a purpose. Such phenomena are bountifully present = minor [premise].
3. Conclusion: There is a supreme Purposer who produces these phenomena through His purposive and ordering activity. From there, we go on to identify this supreme Purposer with the absolute cause of the world to which the ontological and cosmological arguments lead us.

138. On what does this entire teleological argument hinge?

On the truth of the major [premise], which states that there is analogy and concord in the world. This statement cannot be demonstrated, however, but must be presupposed as an axiom, and without it all scientific investigation becomes impossible.

139. Give an overview of the groups to which the phenomena of order and purpose in the world can be reduced.

1. The purely physical laws, such as the laws of gravity, chemical combination, color, origin of musical tones, crystallization, electricity, magnetism, etc. Characteristic of these laws is the fact that they all ⸢are mathematical proportions and⸣[92] can be expressed as mathematical formulas.
2. The purpose and order that manifest themselves in organic beings, both plants and animals. The organs are devised for and adapted to the organism. The entire kingdom of the

92. So DG; omitted in V and A.

organic world is like a great system divided into many smaller kingdoms or systems which in turn break down into even smaller groups. The classification encompasses the whole. Purpose is indispensable also in the physiological processes of growth, reproduction, fertilization, etc.

3. The interaction between body and mind is one of the most poignant examples of purpose. Here we have two different substances united in such a way that they serve each other in even the smallest things. Within the mind itself as well there is a plurality of faculties and powers which nevertheless come together in a single unity.

4. Likewise, a plan or thought manifests itself in social life and in the process of the development of the human race. Individual people each go their own way, without giving much thought to others and the general result. The result is nevertheless such that it achieves a certain common goal. There must therefore be a higher power that governs this historical development. This is where the argument from the philosophy of history has its place.

140. How many groups can you distinguish among the objections which have been leveled against the teleological argument?

The following three:

1. Objections that are hardly adequate, objections that rest on a misunderstanding.
2. Biological objections.
3. Objections that derive from the antiteleological doctrine of evolution.

141. List several inadequate objections and show why they are inadequate.

1. Bacon and Descartes already said that we do not know what the actual purposes of nature are. We respond that our argument does not rest on the claim that we fully know the final purpose of a thing or all things, but only on the claim that

certain things are united with others, like the means with the end. What that end serves, however, is beside the point.

2. It has also been objected that the teleological argument presents humankind as the end of all other creatures, and that this view leads to a most superficial and sentimental view of nature. We respond that teleology has indeed often been developed in this way, especially by rationalists of the popular kind, but that there is no necessary relationship between teleology itself and such abuse of teleology.
3. It has been claimed that the teleological argument only proves how God shapes and rules the world, but not how He creates it. This was the view of Hume, Kant, and John Stuart Mill.[93] We respond:
   a. That the teleological argument does not need to prove more than it can prove. That God is the creator follows from the cosmological argument. Some may claim that the laws and powers by which God shapes the world are so inseparably tied to matter that the one who calls the world into existence can only do so by creating matter. Yet this is a claim that cannot be demonstrated.
   b. It is not natural to recognize God in a dualistic sense as the shaper of the world, and yet to assign matter an independent and eternal existence alongside God. The law of economy demands that we not posit two principles where a single one suffices for explanation. And the fact of the matter is that God does suffice for explanation, since He is quite capable of creating matter.
   c. We also must not overlook the fact that when God uses matter to achieve His purposes, matter has more or less already been made dependent on Him. If it is already partly dependent, no one can object to making it fully dependent—that is, a creation of God.

93. David Hume, *Dialogue Concerning Natural Religion*, ed. Richard H. Popkin, 2nd ed. (Indianapolis: Hackett, 1980); Kant, *Critique of Pure Reason*, 613ff.; John Stuart Mill, *Nature and the Utility of Religion and Theism*, 3rd ed. (London: Longmans, Green, 1885), 167–75.

4. It is said that the wisdom that manifests itself in the order and purposiveness of phenomena is finite, and that one therefore cannot derive from it the conclusion of an infinite (that is, divine), ordered mind. We respond that the teleological argument is not intended in the first place to prove the infinity of God. Moreover, that it cannot be shown that in a sound[94] sense the wisdom that manifests itself in the world is finite.[95]

5. John Stuart Mill claims that every compound of means and end betray finitude and imperfection in the Composer, since He needs the means to achieve the end. We respond that God does not use the means because He cannot achieve the end without them, but simply because He takes pleasure in the beautiful connection between means and end.

6. Finally, people claim that the teleological argument conceives of God as a mechanic who stands outside his work, or as an artist who in similar fashion produces a work of art outside himself. Our response is that there is nothing in the image of an artist that needs to be unworthy of God. We add that God does not stand outside His work like a mechanic or artist, but is at work in the world with His omnipotent power as an immanent God. Finally, that He has Himself created also the matter in and with which He works, which is something a mechanic or artist cannot do.

142. What objection against the teleological argument have people taken from biology, and how should it be countered?

Biology teaches the presence of undeveloped[96] buds of certain organs in certain animals. These are useless and conflict with purposiveness. Our response is:

94. V and A: "sound" (*gezonde*); DG: "grounded" (*gegronde*).

95. V and A: "finite" (*eindige*); DG erroneously reads "infinite" (*oneindige*).

96. V and A: "undeveloped" (*onontwikkelde*); DG erroneously reads: "developed" (*ontwikkelde*).

1. The teleological argument does not claim that every organ and every bud of an organ must serve a specific end.
2. Even though we do not always recognize the use of an organ, it may still have its use.
3. Even though there are many cases in which we can find no teleology, the fact remains that it in many cases remains indispensable.
4. God is not just concerned with purposiveness, but above all with the implementation of classification. It can therefore happen that animals have the buds of certain organs because it was God's will to have them classified in a certain group, even though they cannot make practical use of the organs, for which reason these animals only have those organs in an undeveloped form.

143. What do evolutionary philosophers object against our teleological argument?
That all order and purposiveness, which we think can only be ascribed to the operation of a self-conscious mind, can be explained as the inevitable product of the operation of blind powers and laws. In the past, so it is claimed, people had to make a choice between chance and mind, but now the choice is one between mind and natural causality. Independent scientific laws and powers have been discovered everywhere, which only need to continue working so as to produce, from themselves (without mind), the order and purposiveness manifesting themselves to us in the world.

144. What question do we need to ask and answer in this debate?
The question is not whether there is truth in the doctrine of evolution, but whether it can explain the phenomena of order and purposiveness without the aid of teleology.[97]

97. V and A: "teleology" (*teleologie*); DG: "theology" (*theologie*).

145. How can you show that the doctrine of evolution does not deprive the teleological argument of its power?
By recalling that the form of our argument does not in any way touch upon the way in which the end is realized. We argue from the presence of purposive phenomena to the presence of a purposive mind. How that purposive mind achieved its end was entirely beyond the scope of the discussion. Our argument was an argument by the principle of analogy.

146. Explain this with an example.
If we produce something purposive outside of us with our body as means, and someone then sees this product, that person will rightly conclude that there was a mind which designed and produced it. Yet it is still possible to say that this product has come entirely through natural powers and laws, since our body used purely mechanical power to put it together. Evolutionists, however, want to conclude that there is no ordering mind behind the mechanical powers shaping and developing the world into a beautiful cosmos.

147. To what degree could one still claim that the doctrine of evolution has changed the teleological argument?
Insofar as it now seems unnecessary to locate God in the world as [an] immanent [being]. The powers and laws of nature themselves suffice to lead to the envisioned end. It thus seems as if we can locate God outside the world, as the deists do.

148. Does it just seem this way, or is there more to this argument?
No, for the doctrine of evolution does not explain why the laws of nature work and will continue to work as they do. A law of nature is nothing but an abstraction, it is not something that has independent existence. And so we must once again appeal to the immanent activity of God in order to explain that the laws of nature work as they do and will always work as they do. For none of these laws of nature is it possible to prove a logical necessity. All the simple principles of the doctrine of evolution bear the mark of accidentality and therefore demand a rational ground for explaining their existence.

149. In what respect could the doctrine of evolution perhaps serve to fortify the teleological argument?

1. To the degree that it, by reducing all phenomena to the greatest possible unity, would exclude all multiplicity of governors for this world. Teleology on its own could perhaps still be consistent with polytheism; teleology in combination with evolution cannot.

2. Evolution teaches that the many and heterogeneous have come from the simple. Now the essence of the evolutionary doctrine resides in this, that it brings the many together into a unity. Here then also lies the fact that the production of the many from the one can only have been a work of the mind.

150. What explanations have people sought to give for the order and purposiveness in the world?

1. From the side of the materialists, people have appealed to chance. Under such chance, [so they say,] the world's elements have become interconnected in innumerable ways. One of these innumerable ways, which have usually led to chaotic confusion, is the present connection we find in the world, which in turn has led by pure chance to an ordered result. Of course, chance in this sense of the term is no explanation. Should one shake all the composing parts of a watch countless times, a watch would never—not once!—be the result.

2. People have also appealed to the concept of the laws of nature. A law of nature is in the first place a pure abstraction. It is not something that actually exists. Or, even if one wants to turn it into a metaphysical reality, it is still a blind, senseless reality that cannot explain the purposiveness and order of its own operations. Or, should we want to go yet another step further and ascribe also mind to this metaphysical reality, we would arrive at polytheism. And if we wanted to turn the various laws of nature into a self-conscious law, we would arrive at theism.

3. It has been proposed that purposiveness does not exist in

the things outside of us, but is only the subjective form by which we consider them. This is the view of Kant, which of course relates closely to the subjective-idealist orientation of his entire philosophy. Our response is that we cannot follow this subjectivizing tendency, and that in the event Kant's assumption (i.e., that we find purposiveness everywhere) were correct, we would have to conclude that things are also arranged purposively everywhere. However, Kant's assumption is not correct. In some things we do find purposiveness, in others we do not. This is proof that purposiveness is objective, not subjective.

4. The theory of immanent and unconscious purposiveness. This is the explanation of Hegel, Schopenhauer, and Hartmann.[98] Hegel had pointed out two points of difference between the products of nature and the products of art: (a) In the case of a work of art, the artist stands outside of it, but in nature he is immanent. (b) One must distinguish between the ends that lie within the product and those that lie outside of it. A machine has its end outside of itself, an organic being within itself. Now Hegel claimed that the teleology[99] of nature consists in its attempt to realize such internal ends unconsciously, that is, that the idea brings itself to realization. We respond by countering that we, too, consider God to work immanently in the world. But He must consciously do it in such a way that no one can offer a comprehensible account of the thesis that the idea brings itself to realization. An idea is an abstraction that can only exist in

98. G. W. F. Hegel, *Hegel's Philosophy of Mind*, trans. W. Wallace and A. V. Miller, ed. Michael Inwood (Oxford: Oxford University Press, 2010); Arthur Schopenhauer, *Die Welt und Vorstellung* (Leipzig: F. U. Brodhaus, 1844); Schopenhauer, *The World as Will and Idea*, trans. R. B. Haldane and J. Kemp, 3 vols. (London: Routledge & Kegan Paul, 1883–86); Eduard von Hartmann, *Philosophie des Unbewussten* (Berlin: Carl Duncker, 1870); Hartmann, *Philosophy of the Unconscious*, trans. William Chatterton Coupland, 3 vols. (New York: Macmillan, 1884); cf. Francis Bowen, *Modern Philosophy from Descartes to Schopenhauer and Hartmann*, 7th ed. (New York: Scribner, 1892).

99. DG and V: "teleology" (*teleologie*); A erroneously reads: "theology" (*theology*).

a thinker. The only purposiveness of which we have knowledge and experience is conscious purposiveness.

5. And this is therefore the one[100] we accept as our account of the phenomena revealing such purposiveness.

VI. A Discussion of the Ethical Argument

151. What are the two functions that some ascribe to the conscience, and how many kinds of arguments do they deduce from it for the existence of God?
Some, like ⸢Schenkel,⸣[101] speak of a religious and a moral function of the conscience, and therefore obtain (1) an ethical and (2) a religious argument.[102]

152. How is the etymology of the word "conscience" used to make this sense plausible?
People claim that the word "conscience" comes from *con* and *scio*, that is, "to know together," with God. This would mean that the conscience gives direct evidence about God. That etymological derivation is probably incorrect, however. *Conscire* quite likely means "to know together with our self," that is, to make a judgment on our own acts as to whether they are good or evil. In our conscience we are thus at once judge and judged, which explains the *con*, "with."

153. What three things must the ethical argument in its narrow sense—i.e., distinct from the religious argument—prove?

1. That God exists.
2. That He holds us accountable.
3. That He Himself is a moral being.

---

100. In all mss., the first half of this initial sentence under point 5 has been written under 4; point 5 therefore begins mid-sentence in the original mss.

101. DG has a blank here.

102. Daniel Schenkel, "Gewissen," in *Real-Encyklopädie für protestantische Theologie und Kirche* (Stuttgart and Hamburg: Rudolf Besser, 1856), 5:129–42.

154. What are we to observe in regard to the conscience as a psychological phenomenon?[103]

1. That it is not a separate faculty in the human being apart from the intellect, will, and emotion. Everything that is a psychological phenomenon belongs to these three. The conscience, too, must belong to one or more of these three.
2. At its core, the conscience belongs to the intellectual faculty, and, more specifically, to the faculty of judgment. This is not, however, meant to deny that it can be joined with emotions or exercise influence on the will. The conscience is a judgment on things that are of the greatest importance to us, to which our emotion and will cannot remain indifferent.
3. The conscience is a function or judgment of the intellect with a very specific predicate—namely, good and evil. Knowledge of these two predicates is innate to us as a natural discernment, that is, an *idea innata*. We know immediately what is good and what is evil.

155. What different views are there on the origin and content of these predicates?

1. Some say that they mean nothing less than good = commanded by God, and evil = forbidden by God. The ground on which we call something good would then be the abstract thesis that God commanded it, and the other way around for evil. Our objection to this view is that our conscience does not simply teach that it must do a thing because God commanded it, but in the first place that the thing is in itself good or evil, and that we are for that reason bound by God to do or refrain from doing that thing.
2. A more correct view appears to be the following: Our intellect makes a judgment as to whether a thing is good or evil. It recognizes that "good" refers to what agrees with an absolute norm or standard outside of us, and "evil" to what conflicts with it. Finally, it recognizes that we are bound to

103. A ends here, after Q. 154.

act in accordance with this norm and that we must expect punishment when we refrain from doing so. But if we take the word "conscience" in a narrower sense and understand by it the *actus* of the judging intellect, it must be said that the conscience does presume and include the existence of God, but is not itself the source of an independent knowledge of the existence of God. If we understand "conscience" as everything included under number 2 above, it of course becomes immediate evidence for the existence of God. One should remember, however, that the element that places us in our moral consciousness directly before God and causes us to feel our responsibility to Him, flows from the idea of God that is already innate in us *apart from* it.

156. Is the ethical argument altogether independent of the philosophical theories that have been construed for the origin of the conscience?
No, for if these theories are true, the conscience can and must be explained without taking account of the existence of God.

157. With which three great ideas does ethics occupy itself?

1. The idea of duty.
2. The idea of the good.
3. The idea of virtue.

158. In how many ways can one derive from the conscience and moral consciousness in general an argument for the existence of God and for His moral[104] *existence and our accountability?*

1. By showing that wherever our mind expresses a judgment on all our deeds, it recognizes a judge over us and thus points out that we are not our own masters.
2. By showing that the idea of the good and its opposite, which is innate in us, points, like every idea does, to the existence of a being outside of us in which it has its reality and foundation. An idea cannot hang in the air, but must be reality.

104. V: "moral" (*zedelijk*); DG: "rational" (*redelijk*).

3. By showing that the awareness of incurring punishment, which is linked in us to the doing of evil, in the same way points to a moral[105] being that maintains its moral[106] nature against transgressors.
4. By showing that doing good is for us always connected to a certain sense of satisfaction, and that this cannot be by chance, but must have been arranged teleologically by someone who is the highest good itself.
5. By showing that our conscience in many cases recognizes good and evil as being good and evil immediately, without any reasoning or deliberation. This immediate operation of the conscience, too, bears a teleological mark. We choose the good or the evil as good or evil without knowing why ourselves, and yet our judgment seldom errs.

159. What is the first philosophical view on the origin of the conscience that we need to reject here?
The view of Schopenhauer, which discards the notion of duty.[107] This theory is not adequate since it simply denies the fact instead of explaining it. Schopenhauer argues that one can only say of human beings that they are good or evil, but that it makes no more sense to tell them they must be good than to tell them they must be beautiful. People are beautiful or ugly; on that point there is no "must."

160. What is the theory of Hobbes and Bain?
That the idea of duty has its origins in civil justice.[108] Originally all human beings lived in a barbaric situation, a war of all against all. Later on, some ceded their power to a government, since they saw that no one

105. V: "moral" (*zedelijk*); DG: "rational" (*redelijk*).

106. V: "moral" (*zedelijk*); DG: "rational" (*redelijk*).

107. Arthur Schopenhauer, *On the Basis of Morality*, trans. E. F. J. Payne (Indianapolis: Hackett, 1995), 148–61.

108. Thomas Hobbes, *Leviathan: with Selected Variants from the Latin Edition of 1668*, ed. Edwin Curley (Indianapolis: Hackett, 1994), pt. 2, ch. 28 (pp. 106–9); Alexander Bain, *Mental and Moral Science*, 3rd ed. (London: Longmans, Green, 1872), 1:392–95.

was safe in such a barbaric situation. This government punished every transgression. The result was a fear of punishment, so that people slowly began to feel this fear of punishment as a kind of duty to do the good. They forgot what the origin of this sense of duty was, and began to see it as something independent.

161. What objections do you have against this theory?

1. We feel that we are bound to do also the things that the civil government does not require of us. Our sense of duty is thus much wider than this theory makes it out to be.
2. The original state of the human race is not one of such a barbaric situation, a war of all against all. The family existed before the individual did, before the state. In the family there already existed moral[109] relationships of authority, duty, etc., which therefore do not require an explanation that takes its point of departure from the notion of civil justice.
3. It is absurd to assume that the civil justice system of the state originated from a voluntary contract between individuals. The state was not made, but developed naturally from the family. And when the state later had to maintain itself by coercion and punishment, no one voluntary placed themselves under the state's authority or helped to bring the state into existence.

Utilitarian or Hedonistic Theory

162. What is the utilitarian or hedonistic theory, and who has developed it in ancient and modern times?

The word "utilitarian" (from *utilis*, "useful") means "what proceeds from utility." A theory is utilitarian if it claims that a moral act is good or evil, not because it intrinsically has that character, but simply because it produces good results and is useful, or the opposite.

The word "hedonistic" (from *hedone*, "pleasure") means "what proceeds from pleasure." A theory is hedonistic if it claims that a moral act

109. V: "moral" (*zedelijk*); DG: "rational" (*redelijk*).

is good or evil, not because it intrinsically has that character, but simply because it produces pleasure or pain immediately or eventually.

From this it follows that every hedonistic theory is also utilitarian, although conversely not every utilitarian theory needs to be hedonistic. The decisive question here is how a utilitarian understands the notion of utility, since everyone will soon be left asking why and to what end a thing is useful. Hedonists already answer this question when they say that something is useful for deriving pleasure from it. The utilitarian theory is less specific on this question.

Ancient utilitarians included Aristippus from the Cyrenaic school, as well as the Epicureans; in modern times there are Hobbes, Paley (d. 1805), Bentham (d. 1832),[110] and John Stuart Mill.[111]

163. What do you understand by egotistic hedonism?

The theory that locates the norm for moral good in the pleasure of the agent, such that the agent considers what will bring pleasure to himself and not to others.

164. What do you understand by universalistic hedonism?

The theory that locates the norm for moral good in the greatest possible pleasure for the greatest number of people. Bentham adjusted the theory by introducing the universalist principle.

165. How did John Stuart Mill later change this theory?

He said that one should not just take account of the pleasure of others, but also distinguish between different pleasures. To his mind, there is a difference in kind and not just a difference in degree.[112]

110. DG and V both erroneously read: 1842.

111. Hobbes, *Leviathan*, pt. 1, ch. 13–14 (pp. 74–88); Jeremy Bentham, *The Principles of Morals and Legislation* (Amherst, N.Y.: Prometheus, 1988); John Stuart Mill, *Utilitarianism* (London: Parker, Son, and Bourn, 1863); William Paley, *The Principles of Moral and Political Philosophy*, 8th ed. (Boston: West and Richardson, 1815); cf. Thomas Rawson Birks, *Modern Utilitarianism, or the Systems of Paley, Bentham, and Mill Examined and Compared* (London: MacMillan, 1874).

112. Mill, *Utilitarianism*, 8–37, esp. 10–12.

166. What was the twofold end for which this change was introduced to the theory?

1. To make it appear less harsh and egotistical.
2. To be able to account in some way for the notion of duty.

167. Does the theory really achieve better status when one's own happiness is replaced with the happiness of all?

No, this is just a matter of appearance. If one must do the good for the sake of the happiness and advantage it brings, [the good] is regardless lowered to [the level of] the maidservant of something else and dishonored. According to Bentham, we must seek the good of others as well, not because we have moral[113] duties relating to them, but simply because happiness is the highest thing in the world. If we alone lived in the world, we would be equally moral[114] and good if we sought only our own happiness.[115]

168. What must be observed in regard to the change which John Stuart Mill introduced to the theory?

That it changes the theory radically and thus overturns the utilitarian principle. When I say that a distinction must be made between different pleasures, and that the one pleasure is good and the other evil,[116] I recognize the existence of a measure of good and evil outside of pleasure itself. Mill should have indicated what this norm is—that is, the good cannot be explained from pleasure, but is something independent that is added from the outside.

169. What is the utilitarian theory's biggest problem?

It has no explanation for the idea of duty, and cannot tell us why we must pursue happiness. The only possible way would be to demonstrate that

---

113. V: "moral" (*zedelijk*); DG: "rational" (*redelijk*).

114. V: "moral" (*zedelijk*); DG: "rational" (*redelijk*).

115. Bentham, *Principles of Morals and Legislation*, ch. 11 (pp. 131–51).

116. V: "different pleasures, and that the one pleasure is good and the other evil" (*tussen genot en genot, en dat het ene genot goed is en het andere kwaad*); DG: "the one and the other evil" (*tussen het een en het andere kwaad*).

happiness is the only reality in the world to which all others are subordinated, the ideal of all. The Epicureans thus found their happiness ideal realized in the Olympian gods who had no regard for the human race and continued their life in eternal feasts. It goes without saying that we seek our own happiness. That is our natural inclination. But what can require us to pursue the happiness of our fellow man? Not the fact that it is *their* happiness, and much less so that it is our inclination. Happiness is always something personal from which no duties toward others can be derived.

170. How could one attempt to derive the idea of duty from this theory?[117]
By saying that the entire human race is an organism that pursues the happiness of the whole. That it attempts to reach this end by two means: (1) The individual pursuit of happiness in every individual. (2) The conscience, which incites every person to sacrifice a part of his own happiness for the happiness of the whole.

171. Why is also this theory unlikely?
Because the thesis of such human association is philosophically entirely unproved and will not be accepted by the utilitarians, who are largely empiricists. It is only if one accepts the existence of a God who stands above the human race and seeks to achieve His end with them that one can say with right that the human race as a whole pursues a single end and that from this end flow a person's duties toward the others.

172. What other argument has been adduced for the idea of duty on a utilitarian account?
It has been said that my happiness is so intimately connected with the happiness of others that there is no better way for me to foster it than to see to[118] the happiness of those others. But this can never be an argument for personal duty simply because it remains unproved. When I see to the happiness of others, I will indeed be fostering also my

117. DG: "theory" (*theorie*); V: "idea" (*idee*).

118. DG inserts the following (erroneous) suggestion above the words "to see to" (*te zorgen*): "to say??" (*te zeggen??*).

own happiness to some degree, but what still requires investigation is whether I would be fostering my happiness to an even greater degree if I were simply to look after myself. And according to this theory, any act that puts an end to every opportunity of happiness for me would be ethically repugnant.

Evolutionary Ethicists

173. What other theory do we finally still need to discuss here?

The theory of the evolutionary ethicists, which in ancient times already had its proponents in the Stoics. Its main characteristics are:

1. All people have a kind of instinct of sympathy in them, as a result of which they are happy when others are happy and suffer pain when others suffer pain.
2. This instinct was gradually formed as a product of evolution. At first, it was limited to the circle of the family, and only gradually assumed wider dimensions later on. Initially it was only parents who enjoyed pleasure and suffered pain along with their children and vice versa, while remaining indifferent to the lot of those outside the family.
3. This instinct of sympathy gives people a natural inclination to promote the happiness of others, since they are stimulated to this by the happiness they feel along with others, and conversely an inclination to keep others from pain, since they themselves therefore experience that pain. In this way, the idea of duty arose.

174. What must we object to this theory?

1. That it is at bottom egotistical and utilitarian. For when I help or protect others because I myself desire pleasure or fear pain, my motive is egotistical and my act lacks true morality.
2. That the theory therefore actually has no answer to offer to the question why we must do good to others, but only reduces the idea of duty to the idea of an inclination.
3. When the theory responds that one must do the good because the continued existence of society depends on it, one

must go on to ask why it is actually necessary for society to continue to exist. There are only two possible answers to this question: either because I judge its continued existence to be necessary for my happiness (= egotism) or because it has an end outside itself (= theism).

4. The truth is that the principle of sympathy from which this theory departs must already be considered as proof for the presence of moral duties in us toward others which have been placed on us by God, and that in our emotion these duties are recognized by us in the happiness and suffering in which we share.

VII. The Religious Argument

175. What was the purpose of the old argument e consensu gentium (from the agreement of the nations)?
It sought to prove from the fact that all nations have religion and recognize the existence of God that a God really exists.

176. Is this a legitimate argument?
No, such issues cannot be decided by a roll-call vote. Commonness only has value when this commonness is shown to flow out of a necessity common to all.

177. Which two questions can be distinguished here?

1. What religion is as a psychological phenomenon.
2. How religion arose in history.

We will discuss only the first question here, since the second belongs to the field of biblical history and is also treated in the history of religions.

178. When did people begin to study religion as a psychological phenomenon?
Since Kant. Before that time, there was greater attention to the objective reality which is presumed and recognized by subjective religion.

179. What data do we have to determine what religion is or ought to be in psychological terms?

1. Our own observation. If we may possess religion, we should also more or less be able to form a judgment concerning its particularity.
2. The historical manifestation of religion in different times and among different peoples. When we rightly claim that religion is a general phenomenon, a comparison ought to be possible [to determine] what is common to all who have religion, in spite of their differences and particularities. However, in our claims regarding the commonness of religion, we must see to it that we do not make such a claim from the ideal religion as it ought to be, but rather from a minimal [religion] that still requires closer description.
3. Philosophical considerations. The definition of religion deserving preference is the one that best suits our entire theistic worldview and in its turn sheds its light on that worldview.

180. How can we begin our investigation of the psychological characteristics of religion?

1. By noting that religion is something that has a seat in every human soul.
2. By noting that all psychological phenomena can be reduced to three classes: intellect, will, or emotion. Religion must therefore be something in one, two, or all three of these things.

181. Who has declared religion to be a matter of intellect, a form of knowledge?

All speculative trajectories: the gnostics, the scholastics, rationalists, Schelling, and Cousin. But we can think here in particular of Hegel, who declared religion a lower form of knowledge and said that it exhibits the same truth that philosophy raises to [the level of a] concept.[119]

---

119. G. W. F. Hegel, *Lectures on the Philosophy of Religion: The Lectures of 1827*, ed. Peter

Since Hegel considers the universe to be nothing but a development of the idea of the concept, everything—including religion—must in the end be a conceptual thing, a knowing or representing. This was the position attacked by Schleiermacher, who equally opposed the view of Kant, which holds every religion to be merely a question of the will.[120] As we will see, however, through this twofold critique Schleiermacher fell into the opposite extreme and turned religion into a matter of pure emotion.

182. What are your objections to this view of religion?

1. It would follow that those who are most cultivated and scientifically minded are also the most religious. This is not the case, however, as the example of the devil shows. We can only say that pure knowledge of God is necessary for a pure religion, and that there is no religion that altogether lacks all knowledge of God.
2. It would deprive religion of all possible elements of emotion and will: reverence, veneration, subjection, etc.
3. When Scripture says that knowing God is life eternal,[121] it is referring to a practical knowledge that includes the will and emotion, and also [means] that will and emotion cannot operate in the way of true religion if there is no true knowledge of God.

183. What is the opposite view?

The one that locates the seat of religion in emotion. Epicurus, Lucretius, and Hume located its origin in fear: *Primus timor*[122] *in orbe fecit Deos* (Fear first made the gods on earth). According to Schleiermacher,

---

C. Hodgson, one-volume ed. (Berkeley: University of California Press, 1988), 144–88. Cf. Herman Bavinck, *Reformed Dogmatics*, vol. 1, *Prolegomena*, ed. John Bolt, trans. John Vriend (Grand Rapids: Baker Academic, 2003), 255–58.

120. Friedrich Schleiermacher, *Christian Faith: A New Translation and Critical Edition*, trans. Terrence N. Tice, Catherine L. Lesley, and Edwina Lawler (Louisville, Ky.: Westminster John Knox, 2016), §15 (vol. 1, pp. 116–19).

121. Cf. John 17:3.

122. DG erroneously reads: *orbit*.

religion is an emotion or feeling[123] of absolute dependence, of total passivity.[124]

184. What is the question we are asking, and what are we not asking?

We are not asking whether every religion includes an element of emotion, but whether the core and essence of religion is to be located in emotion, independent of intellect and will.

185. What must we object to the above view?

1. That a religion of pure emotion has never existed and cannot exist. There always was and is an objective reality, or something that is perceived as real by the intellect, to which emotion then reacts.
2. Emotion is awareness of our own situation as being either agreeable or disagreeable. If religion were nothing but emotion, it would become a matter of happiness, something purely hedonistic.
3. A feeling of absolute dependence is no longer a pure emotion. Dependence is a relationship, and a relationship can only be recognized by the intellect. For that reason, Schleiermacher's feeling of dependence is more than emotion, it is an emotion and a recognition of dependence.
4. If religion were emotion, one of two things would have to follow: either all emotion would be religion (which is absurd), or only a certain kind of emotion would be religion. But in the latter case, there would have to be an objective norm by which religious and nonreligious emotions can be distinguished. That is, what is characteristic of religion is once again located in something objective, and not in the subjective emotion as such.

---

123. The Dutch term *gevoel* is used both for the faculty of *emotion* (alongside the intellect and will) and for what in English scholarship on Schleiermacher is generally referred to as the "*feeling* of absolute dependence."

124. Schleiermacher, *Christian Faith*, QQ. 3–4 (vol. 1, pp. 8–27).

186. How did Schleiermacher come to locate the seat of religion in feeling or emotion?

This was related to his pantheistic worldview, which allows no distinction and interaction between the finite and infinite, but makes the infinite and absolute into everything and the finite into nothing. God, the infinite one, cannot become an object for us, for if He did, it would imply an antithesis negating His infinity. But the fact of the matter is that emotion is one such thing through which we become aware of the infinite, not as an object facing us, but rather as the foundation of our own life; it is subjective and passive. It should be clear, however, that this does not suit the definition [of religion] as a feeling of absolute dependence. By saying that we are dependent on the absolute, we have actually already placed the absolute in a certain relationship to us.

187. Can the will be excluded from religion?

No, what distinguishes all pure religion from an unhealthy ⸢pietism⸣[125] is that it works on the will and brings it into sound motion. Religion would not have been able to work on morality to the degree that it did if it had bypassed the will.

188. What argument against the above view can we draw from history?

1. Religion is not at its purest where the element of thought is given a modest role and emotion is placed in the foreground. We rather find lower religious development chiefly among savage tribes. Plato, by way of contrast, occupies a much higher religious position as a result of his intellectual work.
2. History proves that pure knowledge of God is most intimately related to religion itself. The Christian church would not have been so shocked by the doctrinal controversies from which its doctrine developed if it had not sensed and recognized that its entire religion stands or falls with its doctrine. In this position, it was not motivated by a purely speculative

125. DG has a blank here.

interest, but rather by a persistent practical recognition of the relationship between doctrine and religion.

189. What do we need to observe about the derivation of religion from fear?

1. Fear in the strict sense of the term has never produced a religion. Fear is always mixed with an element of reverence and awe. On its own, fear serves better to account for atheism than it does for religion.
2. Fear is unthinkable without the recognition of an object feared. Therefore, here, too, we need to take account of the element of knowledge.
3. Not all fear is religious fear. There must therefore be an objective characteristic by which religious fear can be distinguished from other kinds of fear.

190. What element of truth does this view still have?

The fact that human recognition of God has become servile and fearful through sin.

191. Who has given religion its seat in the will, or considered it a product of the will?[126]

Mansel adds to Schleiermacher's feeling of absolute dependence the awareness of moral duty and locates the essence of religion in both.[127]

Schenkel views the conscience as a religious organ for communion with God.[128]

---

126. Cf. H. D. M. Spence, Joseph S. Exell, Charles Neil, eds., *Thirty Thousand Thoughts Being Extracts Covering a Comprehensive Circle of Religious and Allied Topics* (New York: Funk & Wagnalls, 1889), 143; Robert Flint, *Theism*, 2nd ed. (Edinburgh: William Blackwood, 1878), 346.

127. Henry Longueville Mansel, *The Limits of Religious Thought Examined in Eight Lectures*, 5th ed. (London: John Murray, 1867), 73–94; cf. B. B. Warfield, review of *The Religious Aspect of Evolution*, by James McCosh, *The Presbyterian Review* 9, no. 35 (1888): 510–13.

128. Schenkel, "Gewissen," 129–42.

Kant describes religion as "the fulfillment of our duties as God's commands."[129]

According to Feuerbach, religion merely expresses the desire of people to imagine their own nature as they want it to be.[130]

Strauss combines the views of Epicurus, Schleiermacher, and Feuerbach in his construction of religion.[131]

192. What two groups can be identified here?

1. One group of theories that turns religion into morality, or an extension of morality. Mansel, Schenkel, Kant, etc.
2. A group of theories that locates the origin of religion in an irrational or morally neutral function[132] of the will. Feuerbach and Strauss.

193. What should we observe against the view that religion is morality or an extension of morality?

1. That it deprives religion of its own significance. It is only through religion in its true sense that our moral consciousness becomes complete. But if religion is considered to be something nonindependent, which cannot be distinguished from moral consciousness, there is the risk of isolating[133] this moral consciousness and of reducing religion to a subjective delusion. This happened in Fichte, for example, and the outcome was his atheism.
2. When religion is made to depend on morality, it, too, gets dragged along with various philosophical theories on ethics,

---

129. This phrase from Kant also appears in Q. 35.6, albeit without quotation marks; see the note there.

130. Ludwig Feuerbach, *The Essence of Christianity* (New York: Barnes and Noble, 2004).

131. David Friedrich Strauss, *The Old Faith and the New: A Confession*, trans. Mathilde Blind, 2nd ed. (London: Asher, 1873).

132. V: "an irrational or morally-neutral function" (*e. onredelijke of zedel. neutrale functie*); DG: "an immoral or moral-neutral function" (*een onzedelijke of zedelijke-neutrale functie*).

133. DG: "of isolating" (*te isoleren*); V erroneously reads: "to" (*tot*).

and as the ethical concepts change, the view on religion will have to be adjusted accordingly. Viewed apart from the light of religion, the moral life is something so mysterious and inexplicable that one could never find an acceptable explanation for it.

3. From a historical perspective, religion always precedes morality. Already in the earliest times we do not find religion flowing from morality, but conversely being what actually gives morality its power and bolsters it.

194. What is Feuerbach's particular view on religion?

He initially belonged to the school of Hegel. Later he left it and developed a system of anthropologism. According to it, all supernatural representations that we form for ourselves are a product of our own imagination. In our gods, we worship our own nature as we would want it to be. We create a god for ourselves after our own image and likeness. People do not, however, know that they are actually worshiping themselves in the gods created thus. This is where the immoral effect of religion is located. We imagine that we are serving and loving another, but in reality we serve and worship ourselves in purely selfish fashion.

195. How would you criticize this theory?

1. Religion as it has been worked in humankind by the grace of God is not selfishness. In the Christian's heart, an act of self-surrender truly does take place.

2. Ever since sin's entrance into the world, all natural religion has indeed had such an element of self-worship. Where Feuerbach goes wrong, however, is in his assumption that this is the original and normal state of things. But it is actually something abnormal, pointing rather to the necessity of true religion. Since the human race is constituted for religion, it must have something to worship and venerate. Where people fall away from God, they are forced to turn themselves and the world into a God. As such, this self-worship contains within itself an argument for the reality of religion.

196. How are we to answer the question of what religion is?

1. By saying that religion does not just pertain to a single faculty of the soul, but extends at once to the intellect, will, and emotion. Religion depends on all three, and in all three of these spheres it depends on its purity in the other spheres. The purer religious knowledge is, the better—all other conditions being equal—shall be the will and the more sacred emotion. Of course, this does not mean that knowledge on its own suffices to make the will religious or to incline it toward God. If you take two people who both have their will inclined toward God, you will still have to say that the one in whom religious knowledge is purest and greatest will also have a will evincing more religious energy.

2. With regard to the essence of religion it must be said that it consists in our finite being's determination by the infinite God, as it comes to expression in our thoughts, words, and deeds—that is, as it is recognized by us.

197. What twofold sense of the word "religion" follows from this?

1. The subjective sense: the recognition of this determination by God.

2. The objective sense: the content of what is being recognized.

Although the term "religious" actually has a subjective significance, it is still good to continue speaking of an objective religion so as to avoid the error of insisting that we are dealing with something purely subjective. Our subjective worship of God depends on our objective recognition of God's existence and His rights.

198. How can the above definition be further developed?

1. Religion is a relationship that presumes a subject and an object.

2. It is a relationship in which the subject (man) and the object (God) do not stand alongside each other as equals, but the former is determined by the latter. The greater the recognition of this [principle], the purer the religion.

3. On the level of the intellect, being "religious" means recognizing God as the ground and source of all truth and resting in Him with our conviction of all truth. This applies to innate ideas as well as experience, and this religious intellectual act or *habitus* of the intellect is called "faith" in the widest sense of the term.
4. On the level of the will, being "religious" means that our soul inclines itself to God as the highest good, that we gladly consider ourselves means existing for God and His glory.
5. On the level of emotion, being "religious" means that we find this devotion to God and His intentions to be our highest pleasure, which through the expressions of our will and the recognition of our intellect is accompanied by a special response in our emotion.

199. Can everything that is considered to be historical religion actually bear this name in view of the ideal of religion?
No, for through sin this ideal religion became something that the human race cannot reach. And even the re-creating grace of God only restores it partially.[134]

200. How can one then still speak of religion where sin has entered?

1. Insofar as some knowledge of God still remains in the human race. People know that God exists and has rights on them which He will certainly exercise. There is thus knowledge of God both without and within the conscience, even though this knowledge is no longer pure knowledge of God.
2. The sovereignty of God as it is recognized makes its influence felt on the will as well. But this is not because we in the core of our will subject ourselves to God and consider ourselves means to His ends, but simply because our selfish motives prevent us from being so bold as not to obey Him at all. The

134. This question and answer is omitted in DG.

conscience is therefore a cognitive faculty, and it gains influence on the will by selfish motives.

3. The religion of the unregenerate is therefore a religion that cannot be valid in the eyes of God. What it lacks is the very core.[135]

201. Can religion depart even further from its ideal than described above?
Yes, for knowledge of God can become so corrupt that people end up losing their awareness of a personal, holy God.

202. Does some religion still remain in them?
Yes, for even when people fall from their awareness of the existence of a personal God, they cannot fail to set up something else in God's place so as to venerate[136] it. As we have seen above, the simple fact is that people have been constituted to move around some center outside of themselves. Even after losing God as their center and becoming self-centric, people still find themselves under the power of their original inclination to the degree that they must find a new center that is—to their mind, at least—outside of themselves. They do so by placing their *ego* outside of themselves and now venerating it as something objective.[137] All idolatry therefore contains an element of self-worship. See also what has been remarked above against the theory of Feuerbach. See also Romans 1:25.

203. What follows from this description[138] of religion?
The widespread manifestation of religion now obtains a new significance. We have found an explanation for it. Religion is a general phenomenon, since it is necessary for the human race and belongs to its nature. Modified in this way, the argument *e consensu gentium* has validity.

---

135. So V; omitted in DG.

136. V: "venerate" (*vereeren*); DG: "fear" (*vreezen*).

137. DG: "objective" (*objectiefs*); V erroneously reads: "subjective (*subjectiefs*).

138. DG: "description" (*beschrijving*); V: "distinction" (*onderscheiding*).

204. How must this religious argument be related to the aforementioned arguments?

Not so much as a new or separate argument for the existence of God, but as the living summary of the different arguments. All the things that have been argued abstractly above now show themselves to be a practical reality in the lives of people, which they must and do indeed take into account.

THE IMMORTALITY OF THE SOUL

205. What question must we first address before we can speak about the immortality of the soul?

The question concerning the essence of the soul. We must first consider what the soul is. If, for example, one considers it to be material, it will no longer be of use to assign immortality to it. Conversely, if the soul is what we claim it to be, its immortality becomes more than merely probable.

206. What four theories or hypotheses are there concerning the essence of the soul?

1. The materialist view, which declares the soul to be a product of the corporeal organism.
2. The idealist view, which holds the individual soul to be a function or manifestation of a more deeply seated, spiritually independent entity, while denying it individuality and personal consciousness.
3. The identity thesis, which views the soul and body as two sides of a third entity, which is neither mind nor matter, but the undivided ground of them both.
4. The dualistic theory, which views the body as an organic composition of material parts in interaction with the soul, which is an absolute unity, an immaterial independent entity.[1]

207. Which two forms can the materialist view assume?

1. It can turn the soul into a second, materially independent entity apart from the body.
2. It can turn the soul into a function of the corporeal organism, such that it cannot be called independent in the strict sense of the term.

1. V: "independent entity" (*zelfstandigheid*); DG: "substance" (*substantie*).

Virtually no one currently adheres to the first form of the theory; in antiquity, however, it did have its proponents. These days almost everyone opts for the second view.

208. How can you criticize this second form?
We must point out that one of our very first and most fixed convictions is that matter and mind differ *toto genere* and therefore cannot ever pass into each other. All our thinking and speech is adapted such that it no longer makes sense for someone to say that "brains think" or "thinking is motion."

209. Why is it impossible to say that thinking is a function of the brain as digestion is a function of the stomach?
Because the word "function" in this example simply means a series of material operations by the organ. The function thus remains always within the material sphere. Thought as a function of the brain, however, would be something of new class occurring in an altogether different sphere. The separation of gall is a function of the liver, but it is possible to find the gall in the liver ahead of time using material means. No one, however, can find thought in the brain.

210. How is it that so many persist in adhering to materialist views on the nature of the soul in spite of this objection?
This flows from the fact that we can only perceive the soul in its connection with the body. We never perceive the soul anywhere without the body, even though we do believe that it can exist without the body. It develops together with the body. In fact, the two are parallel. Materialists appeal to these phenomena when they declare the soul to be a function of the body. From the correlation of soul and body they conclude that the former is nothing but a function of the latter. This is not a legitimate conclusion to draw, however. Yet it may well be that the soul, to the degree that we can perceive it, always uses our brain to think. However, it does not follow in any way that thinking is merely a function of the brain.

211. What does the idealistic theory claim, and how would you criticize its psychology?
It declares the individual soul to be a manifestation of the undivided, unconscious substance that lies behind it and alone possesses immortality. Our criticism is that the soul forms a strictly indissoluble unity, so that it cannot be a manifestation of something else and still be unconscious and undivided. There can be no substantial unity between multiple souls.[2]

212. What does the identity thesis claim, and what can we observe against it?
The material and mental phenomena in a person form two series in which a third substance unknown to us manifests itself. The two series do not depend directly on each other; there is no immediate interaction between body and soul. But through the third [substance], of which both are manifestations, a certain parallelism is in place. Our objections to this view are as follows:

1. We know mind and matter to be distinguished in such a way that they cannot be united into a higher unity as phenomena. No one can form a conception of this third thing. Moreover, we must also say *a priori* that it is an impossible concept that attempts to unite conflicting attributes within itself.
2. It would follow from this hypothesis that the parallelism between mind and matter, soul and body, must be complete. In other words, it would follow that there is no corporeal phenomenon that is not accompanied by a psychological phenomenon, and vice versa. ⸢This, however, brings the hypothesis into all kinds of problems.⸣[3] The image of a table, for example, thus corresponds to the table in the material sphere. However, in my mind there is not just the image of the table, but also the awareness that I have that image. What, then, corresponds to the latter in the material sphere? This question can be repeated into infinity.

2. This question and answer are omitted in V (error by homoioarcton).
3. So V; omitted in DG.

3. We have an awareness of causality in our inner life, that is, we sense[4] immediately that our soul operates on our body. If the identity thesis were correct, it would mean that this awareness of causality is an illusion.

4. Even so we can convince ourselves at any moment how the body operates directly on the soul.

213. Give a brief summary of the fourth, dualistic theory.
According to it:

1. Mind and matter are substances of different classes, which can never pass into each other or be mixed substantially.

2. Mind and matter, soul and body, still work on each other as we daily experience it.

3. This operation of one substance on the other does not occur by the transfer of physical power in the soul or a psychic power on the body, but in a way that is altogether incomprehensible to us. Nevertheless, the operation [of the one on the other] is real; the soul truly is the cause of the body's movement, and not a mere *causa occasionalis* (occasional cause), and vice versa.

214. Does the law of the persistence of energy not contain an insuperable objection against this theory?
No.

1. Because the law of the persistence of energy remains an unproved hypothesis.

2. Even if we were to accept its validity, it would only have to mean that an equivalent would have to come in the place of every physical energy. [It would] not [necessarily demonstrate] that the sum of all physical energy in the world would always have to remain the same. It would indeed be possible

4. DG: "we sense immediately" (*we nemen onmiddelijk waar*); V erroneously reads: "we assume immediately" (*we nemen onmiddelijk aan*).

through the operation of souls on bodies for new physical energy to remain persistent from that moment onward.

3. Even if we were to accept the extreme (i.e., that the sum total of physical energy in the world must always remain the same), in an unfathomable, metaphysical way the soul can still set the physical energy present in the body in motion without any physical energy being transferred to the body or the sum total of physical energies in the world increasing.
4. In no case may the law of the persistence of energy be understood such that physical energy can be transformed into mental energy and vice versa.

215. How does this theory further describe the soul?

As a complete unity manifesting itself in our self-consciousness. Consciousness and self-consciousness are for us the inalienable mark of the concept of the soul. Conscious life may indeed be interrupted temporarily through sleep, but when I wake up, I am once again conscious of my identity.

216. How would you describe the immortality of the soul involved here?

As the continued existence, even after the body's decomposition, of the soul as the indivisible subject of mental phenomena, where this subject remains conscious of its own identity throughout all circumstances. There are therefore two elements to which one must pay careful attention: (a) the identity of the substance; (b) the permanence of the consciousness of this identity.

217. How is the immortality of the soul, understood in this sense, to be distinguished from other views on it?

1. Theologically, immortality is understood as the mental state of the soul when it participates in God's unfailing communion and therefore acts in full harmony with all its energy and faculties. In this sense, no sinner has the immortality of the soul.
2. Pantheistic-philosophically, the immortality of the soul

means nothing other than that the soul, at the death of the body, returns to the impersonal,[5] unconscious, spiritual substance of which it was a manifestation. This means that it is not absolutely destroyed. We, of course, have a much bigger understanding of immortality than simply the nondestruction of the soul.

218. What is the metaphysical argument for the immortality of the soul?
It proceeds as follows: death is always a dissolution and separation of parts; the soul is a perfect unity in which no parts are found; its dissolution is therefore impossible; it is immortal.

219. What must we object?

1. That the soul cannot be divided or separated does not prove in any way that it is indestructible. If it were destroyed, it would be difficult to claim that it is immortal in the above sense of the term.
2. That the argument only becomes persuasive once it has been demonstrated that the soul is not destroyed.

220. How could one demonstrate that the soul is not destroyed?
By analogical reasoning, and by pointing out that, as far as we can perceive it, nothing in this world is ever destroyed. Furthermore, by pointing out that the soul, if it continues to exist, must continue existing with the attributes that belong specifically to it, that is, as an individual, self-conscious, mentally independent entity.

221. What is the weakness in this metaphysical argument?
Its inability to claim decisively that nothing in the world is destroyed. The death of animals presents us with a problem. Is their mind destroyed? Or are there reasons to accept that their soul is an indivisible unity?

5. V: "impersonal" (*onpersoonlijke*); DG: "original" (*oorspronk.*).

222. In how many forms has the ethical argument for the immortality of the soul been presented?

1. It has been said that humankind's moral nature demands an infinite progression so as to approach the ideal of moral perfection. A future life that never ends would thus be a postulate of our moral nature. This is the argument used by Kant in his *Critique of Practical Reason*.[6] We counter:

   a. That it may be true that complete moral goodness is demanded of us, but that it is not true that it must be approached through an infinite process. Moral perfection is not infinite in this philosophical sense of the term.

   b. In their sinful, fallen state, people cannot expect that such an infinite perfection will be given them. It is demanded of them, but through their sin they have lost their right to it and therefore cannot expect an eternal existence on the basis of a nonexistent right. If human beings were destroyed, their rights would not be violated. Since people do not move toward the ideal of moral perfection but rather place themselves at an ever greater distance from it, their destruction would even prevent a greater defect.

   c. It is in the regenerate alone that a principle of eternal life, which is able to develop itself, can be found. However, natural theology cannot account for regeneration, since it belongs to the sphere of grace.

2. A second form of the ethical argument, which likewise appears in Kant, proceeds from the eudaemonistic thesis that virtue and happiness ought always to accompany each other. In the present life that is not the case. Therefore, there must be a future life in which that does happen. We object:

   a. That we can make no claim on happiness as a reward for our virtue. Every reward occurs *ex pacto*, that is, according to the free promise of God, by agreement, even though it does remain true that the possession of virtue gives an inner satisfaction that cannot be separated from it.

6. Kant, *Critique of Practical Reason*, 102–3.

b. That this form of the argument does not prove an eternal, continued existence of the soul. Who might say how long or short a period of happiness must be if it is a reward for our virtue?

3. A third form of the ethical argument is more adequate. It proceeds from our awareness of our responsibility and of our incurring punishment. Our conscience tells us that God is just and that our sin is deserving of eternal punishment.

223. *What is the religious argument for the immortality of the soul?*
It proceeds from the assumption that the human race stands in a moral and mental position *vis-à-vis* God and is conscious of that position. Now it would be absurd for God to enter into a close relationship of ⸢solidarity⸣[7] and community with a creature that is destined to disappear as individual. In other words, the fact that the human race is God's image bearer makes the supposition of the ending existence of the soul an improbable one. The same can be concluded from the fact that the *a priori*, innate truths extend humanity's knowledge beyond experience.

224. *What is the ground for the historical argument for the soul's immortality?*

1. The conviction that all accept immortality, to which one might object by pointing to the undemonstrated nature of the thesis and by noting that the common manifestation of a thing does not as such prove its truth.
2. The claim that spiritual[8] manifestations have taken place. The point here is that the evidence for such phenomena must be weighed. In Scripture we have certain historical

7. DG has an ellipsis here.

8. Vos is presumably referring to the appearance of spiritual beings (i.e., angels), as attested in Scripture. It should be noted that the noun *geest*, which has been translated adjectivally here as "spiritual," has been rendered throughout the rest of this translation as "mind" or "mental."

proofs[9] for such a reality. As pure history, these fall under the data[10] of natural theology.

3. On the fact of Christ's resurrection, one of the most clearly demonstrated facts from all of world history.

End.
September 27, 1898. L. J. Veltkamp
Grand Rapids, Michigan[11]

---

9. V: "we have certain historical proofs" (*hebben wij zekere historische bewijzen*); DG: "we indeed have historical proofs" (*hebben wij zeker historische bewijzen*).

10. V: "data" (*gegevens*); DG: "history" (*historie*).

11. DG: *13 April 10 PM 95.*
Grands Rapids Mich.
W. de Groot.

Board of the Dutch Reformed Translation Society

INDEX